LIFE Lift

**OVERCOME
EVERY LIMITATION
TO ELEVATE YOUR
LIFE AND UNLEASH
YOUR DREAMS**

D1052541

REX CRAIN

ISBN: 978-1-890900-58-8
Library of Congress catalog card number: 2010942561

Printed in the United States of America.

CONTENTS

ACKNOWLEDGMENTS

To the most wonderful God, thank you for your grace and patience, and for allowing me to become and experience more than I imagined possible or deserved. Your favor has changed me to be the person I always wanted to be!

To Katrina, the woman of my dreams and best friend. Thank you for inspiring me. Your unconditional love and positive spirit have made me the man I am today. I love you!

To Dad and Mom, thank you for your love, encouragement, and investment, from the Little League practices to the airport runs. Your unfailing love has shown me how to love and embrace what matters most in life. I love you!

To Grandpa and Grandma, thank you for always being there. Your legacy of kindness, wisdom, and trust in God have shaped my life. Thank you for believing in me!

To Russell, thank you for being a great brother, from "the Johnny and Roy" days until now. You and Alicia have enriched my life with your friendship.

To the Ojanen family, thank you for your continual love and support. I appreciate you!

To Doug Reeves, I am forever grateful for your investment in my life. Our conversations have stretched me and launched me into God's purpose for my life.

To Tim Storey, your friendship and insight have motivated me to live the Jesus style. You taught me, if He could do it, I could do it. Thank you.

LIFE *Lift*

To John and Linda Mason, your friendship, dedication, hard work, and belief in this book will, in turn, change thousands of people's lives. Thank you for you being the best writing and publishing partners a person could have.

To Ben and Erin Figueroa, thank you for your wisdom, belief in me, and help in making this book a reality.

To Brig and Lita Hart, thank you for your friendship and partnership, and for motivating me to write this book.

To David and Mike at MRKd.TV, thank you for believing in this project. I greatly appreciate your effort.

To my friends and supporters, I am grateful that you enable me to help millions of people. Your love, loyalty, and prayers have impacted the course of history. I am thankful for people like you who believe in the purpose God gave me.

INTRODUCTION

Have you ever thought you're not living up to who you really are? If so, get excited! What you're experiencing is an inner dissatisfaction that says your life can be more than it is, and that desire is there to break you out of your current challenges and lift you into an experience where your greatest potential is unlocked and unleashed.

That desire brought you to this book. Like most people, no matter how challenged you are or how well you're doing, you're in need of a boost called a life lift. A lift is an upward pull that raises a person from a lower to a higher position in their condition. Maybe you need a lift in your physical condition, relationships, or finances. Your life can be elevated and take off in a new direction.

Your path will become great when you factor in divine power, a power that says there's more vision, more victory, and more enjoyment of life and people. That power wants to be tapped, activated, and demonstrated.

Let's journey together as we unlock your highest experience and potential. Let's embrace a life lift.

1

What Once Was

Have you ever wondered if there's more to life than what you're living?

If you're like most people, you found yourself in childhood dreaming about and imagining what you wanted to become, places you wanted to go, and things you wanted to do. But as you grew older, maybe you began to think of the dreams you once dreamed as more of a luxury that you could no longer afford and no longer take time for.

Our dreams become replaced and misplaced due to daily predictability and growing concerns about house payments, food, clothing, and medical bills. After working all day and pushing through the routines of life, it seems like the only dreams we have left are the ones in our sleep. We're exhausted and burned out by obligations that never end, relationships that lack love and luster, and a dissatisfaction inside that says there has to be more to life than this.

On the surface, everything might look good. You might have achieved a certain amount of success relationally and professionally, fulfilling dreams in these areas. You might have the degree you worked hard for, the wife or husband you dreamed of, and annual vacations in Hawaii. Maybe you've thought to yourself, I have a job, a spouse, children, a nice car, and an okay life, and this is enough for me. You've convinced yourself to stop and settle right where you are, at a comfortable place. Like many men and woman before us, we've hit the brakes. Comfort and complacency have replaced passion and purpose.

Help me, I'm stuck

When we settle for comfort, are we really just allowing our bag of excuses and fears to talk us out of attempting something we really desire and dream of doing? Who hasn't thought, I'll probably fail, so why try now when I have too much to lose? Yet, this kind of pessimistic attitude keeps us stuck.

Being stuck is being detained, delayed, confused, and baffled. When we're stuck, life starts to become uneventful and leads to a destiny undone. Off track from our destiny, we live by default rather than by God's design, where we start letting life do something with us rather than us doing something with life.

Not only can we get stuck in fear, but all of us can get stuck in the past; in pictures of things that once were, in stories of what once was. When we get stuck in our memories, we become addicted to a life without dreams. We put them aside because we feel we don't have what it takes to reach the next level.

Maybe your past has made such an impact on your present, you can't even enjoy your now.

Where have you been? Maybe a choice or series of poor choices created challenges; maybe physically you didn't take care of yourself and now you're filled with regret because you find yourself in a body you don't like or feel comfortable in. Or maybe you've received a report from the doctors with little promise of hope or recovery. Maybe you've been through something you swore would never happen to you, like an addiction or a divorce, so now you find yourself bewildered, deflated, and detached from experiencing what you felt life had for you.

Personally, I know what that feels like. At one period in my life, challenges from the personal, relational, and financial sides were uprooting me from a sense of certainty about who I was and what my life was to be about. I began to wonder and question if there would be better days ahead for my life.

I began to see I couldn't stay stuck in that place of feeling sorry for myself, the place of being driven by backward thoughts such as, why didn't this relationship work out? why did this happen? and why does life seem so unfair? It seemed like the whys in my own life were on an assignment to break my will and lock me into a life of defeated attitudes and conversations—a destructive pattern that painted a not-so-bright future.

Feeling overwhelmed by these challenges, I began to think about "checking out." I was looking for a way to escape the feelings of pain and sadness that were festering in my mind, giving me an invitation to check out of my life and out of what I was put on this planet to do.

Thankfully, God showed me what was good about me and revealed some big dreams that awaited my arrival. He brought people into my sphere of pain and defeat to give me a lift. Their voices of hope and wisdom began to fill the canvas of my mind

Without a lift, I hate to think where I'd be today.

with vision and encouragement instead of darkness and confusion. Without a lift, I hate to think where I'd be today. But there was hope for me, and there's hope for you too.

I learned something I want to pass on to you: We can never access what can be, while we're preoccupied with what once was.

Regress, reside, retard

Our lives were designed to go *forward* and *upward*. Life is motion, movement, and advancement. Without advancement and progress, we begin to do what I term as "regress, reside, and retard."

You're *regressing* when you're so overwhelmed by disappointment, hurt, and frustration that you begin to think there's no sense in getting up. You sit in the seat of regret over the life you "could'a, should'a, would'a" had, but never accessed. What once was has you locked in regret over what you could have done but didn't, where you should have been but weren't, what you would have had, but didn't.

If you fall into the category of regressing because of personal and professional setbacks and disappointments, you'll find yourself residing in a life that once was.

You're *residing* when you settle for a life that clings to past accomplishments and embraces present conveniences, all the while compromising your heart's desires. It's a life that will never move forward.

You can identify people who are stuck here by listening to them; they constantly talk about the "good old days." They're always bringing up a high school sports achievement, how they used to look, what they used to do, or what life was like before being stuck in a dead-end job, unsatisfying relationships, and the pressures of daily life. While it's wonderful to enjoy and celebrate a past accomplishment, your spirit will never be satisfied with what you did yesterday.

This became real to me many years ago when my childhood dream became a living reality; I was signed to a professional contract to play baseball for the Boston Red Socks. In my view at the time, this was all I ever wanted to do and all I ever wanted to explore.

But after an encounter with an older woman sitting next to me on a plane to spring training, my life would never be the same. Her name was Louise Hicks, and she asked me if I was really into the book I was reading on my lap. I said, "I'm trying to be." She started to speak to me about the treasure and significance that the book held for my life. She shared, too, how her life had been transformed by reading it and by her relationship with the Author of that book.

If you haven't figured it out, that book was the Bible. In a few short hours, the bright seventy-six-year-old woman began to expand my mind and heart about the rich purpose and plan God had designed for my life.

Up to this point, I had never thought about this; I had always thought of success and fulfillment in terms of what I had done and was doing in baseball. As we conversed, her words of inspiration and empowerment opened me up to a reality of being more than I was. Her words began to bring my heart to life as she described how I would touch millions of people through the gifts of encouragement and wisdom that were inside of me.

As she spoke, I realized I was more than I was living; I could not settle and reside in the place where I currently found myself.

Like me, you can't sit and settle where you are. The potential inside of you demands advancement. If you don't, you run the risk of retarding your life, which means it becomes restricted and dammed up. When restricted like this, all you experience are the constant frustrations of life, regardless of your financial status.

You can't sit and settle where you are.

If your life is *retarding,* without a doubt you're experiencing suspended momentum and movement in your life. This leads to delays and distractions in fulfillment of the life you want to see and experience. This postponement brings a work stoppage to your potential and dreams, which makes the life you desire and deserve seem like it's in a distant place. You're stuck in what once was.

Eat your heart out

A nine-year-old boy was learning about eagles in school. He was learning about how powerful they are, how they can spread their wings up to seven feet wide, and how they have the potential to fly ten thousand feet high. He learned that eagles mate in the air, whereas other flying birds only mate when they're on the ground.

He learned that eagles are able to soar to higher altitudes than other birds, so in a storm, other birds are hiding for shelter while eagles are accelerating and flying above it.

One day, the boy set out to find an eagle. He packed his lunch, grabbed his binoculars, and walked to the park. As the hours passed, he wondered if he would ever see one, but then, there it was! He saw an eagle, and it was everything he'd heard about and more. This was the greatest day of his life!

As he watched the eagle glide, suddenly it turned and swooped downward. It picked something up, but the boy couldn't see what it was. Then the eagle flew back up in the air and began to soar. But then, something happened. Perplexed, the boy watched as the eagle began frantically flapping its wings. Instead of soaring and gliding, the eagle was beating its wings hard.

Suddenly, the eagle began to lose momentum, strength, and height. It had flown very high, but now it began to come crashing down. *Boom!* It hit the ground.

The boy hurriedly ran a few blocks and found the eagle. He thought, what happened—was it shot down by a gun? did its wings hit a wire?

When he lifted a wing, he didn't see any blood from a wound. But when he turned the eagle over, he saw a little weasel on its heart. He began to cry, "You're so smart, so beautiful, and so powerful. Why did you hang on to the weasel? Didn't you know that as long as you held on to it, it would eat your heart out?"[1]

What weasels have you picked up along the way that you are allowing to eat the heart out of your dreams, the heart out of your big life, the heart out of your marriage, the heart out of your relationships, the heart out of your gift?

If you keep hanging on, you will never be able to reach your proper altitude. A plane can't reach its altitude if it has too much baggage on board. You have to know when to let things go. If you don't let them go, they will weigh you down. It's hard to run, it's hard to move, and it's hard to soar when you have to deal with excess baggage and excess weight in your life. If you never release your weasels, you will never soar as high as you were destined to fly.

What weasels have you allowed to eat the heart out of your dreams? As a result, you feel life is passing you by and you wonder, is there more to life than this? There has to be more.

Setbacks

Being stuck is a setback, and a setback is a reversal of progress. Setbacks want us to stay in our then instead of moving into our now, constantly looking back over our rearview shoulder. Looking back distracts us from what our heart really wants, which is the future. We can't be forward people and stuck on backward thoughts.

How do we get stuck in setbacks?

1. We reap what we sow

   Sometimes we sow to win and we reap the whirlwind through a series of bad choices. Although a bad choice can put you in a bad spot, a good choice can get you out of a bad spot.

2. Spiritual opposition

   You have to admit, there's more than meets the eye. Sometimes there are unseen forces that are out to oppose us and unravel our sense of peace, rhythm, and health. These forces can make us feel oppressed and overwhelmed, as if there is no way out of setbacks and current challenges.

3. Bad choices of others

   Sometimes people make bad decisions and someone else becomes a victim of them.

Regardless, these setbacks that occur from time to time are out to neutralize our effect. They can cause each of us to reduce our thinking to how do I survive? and how do I cope? instead of dreaming about what is possible in our lives.

You were not designed to be a survivor; you and I are made in the image of God, and God is not trying to survive. In fact, he is a creator, innovator, and initiator. He designed us to have a divine effect on this planet; a life where we rule, lead, and create. He doesn't want us stuck in regret and shame over past events and the drama of life.

We can get so stuck in our present lives that we stop looking ahead to what possibly can be.

You were not designed to be a survivor; you and I are made in the image of God, and God is not trying to survive.

Michelle

A friend I was helping asked if he could bring his friend to me who was struggling with addictions.

He said she was about to go into the porn industry because of some recurring setbacks she was experiencing, and he felt that I had helped him so much, I might be able to help this girl named Michelle.

He brought her to my office, and we began to talk about life. She told me that her mom died when she was one and that her dad died when she was eleven. She felt like everyone close to her had always abandoned her; she was tired of going through the motions, never getting ahead, and always feeling alone. She told me she was going to go into the porn industry to make some quick money because life had lost meaning.

I asked her, "Before you do that, what do you really want out of life?" She didn't know. I asked, "Did you ever dream about being married?"

She said, "Yes, I'd love to be married. I always thought I'd make an amazing wife." I asked her why she thought that, and she told me, "Well, I always thought I'd be a person who could give love and receive love and be a great companion."

I gave her a piece of paper. "Write that down," I told her. Then I asked, "Did you ever want to have children?"

"I would love to have children," she said. "I think I'd be an amazing mom. In fact, I've always wanted to be a mom. I want to give a child the love I never received from my mom."

I asked Michelle to write that down, too. "Did you want to live in a house? Here in California?"

"I always thought I'd live in a house," she said, and she began to describe it to me. She kept saying over and over, "I always thought…" And all the while, I urged her to write these things on her paper.

As she began to look at the piece of paper, Michelle began to scream and cry. She began to see the reality of what she was pursuing in the light of what she really wanted and what was really important to her. She saw where her life was headed and that it wasn't matching up with what her heart really craved.

She started screaming, "I want my future! This is what I want!" She grabbed the paper and began to sob uncontrollably over it.

I felt that God told me something about her life—that three months earlier, she'd gone through an abortion. He urged me to tell her, "God isn't mad at you over what you did three months ago—your son's in heaven, and you'll see him again someday."

She started screaming even more, and when the tears slowed down, I led her in a prayer to forgive herself and to receive God's mercy, grace, and forgiveness. Then she asked me something really weird: "Would you come to the bathroom with me?"

I said reluctantly, "Uh…sure." I grabbed my friend and said, "You're coming too." The three of us went to the bathroom together, and she opened her purse. She began to hand me needles, heroin, and cocaine.

She said, "I don't want this stuff—I see my *future* and I *want* it!"

She asked me to flush the drugs for her, but I told her, "This is your moment—you need to flush them." She chose to throw away the rags of her shame and clothe herself with dreams for her future that were inspired and renewed by God.

Michelle learned she had to flush out what was toxic so she could flesh out what was timeless. She discovered there was more to her than what she was living; and this discovery unlocked her from what once was in her life. Her future lay beyond the setbacks, the baggage, the disappointments, and challenges she'd experienced in her past.

The same is true for you. This is your moment to unlock the rest of your story. How will you envision the rest of your life taking shape, from this moment forward?

Your dreams fuel your future. This is where you decide, "I'm not going to let the story of what once was define me, defeat me, and detach me from what can be."

2

What Can Be

What can be? Every human being has thought about it.

In the year 1990, Jim Carrey was a struggling actor and comic from Canada, trying to find his way in Hollywood. One day he drove his old Toyota up Mulholland Drive. As he sat there looking out over the city, he began to dream about his future.

In fact, he wrote himself a ten-million-dollar check which he dated Thanksgiving 1995. He added the notation "for acting services rendered," and he carried it in his wallet from that day forward.

His positive outlook helped him lift beyond his personal setbacks and disappointments, and even his bout with depression, until in 1995, he became a huge box office success. Not only did his acting roles in *Ace Ventura: Pet Detective, The Mask,* and *Dumb and Dumber* allow him to earn the ten-million-dollar check he had written to himself, but his asking price rose to 20 million dollars per picture.

Imagine yourself different than you are; your life different than it's been. You're created in the likeness of God from his imagination, so you are created to imagine. If you aren't living out of your imagination, you're malfunctioning.

Your life today is a result of what you thought yesterday, but your life tomorrow will be the result of what you think today. The wisest man who ever lived, King Solomon of Israel, said that as a man "thinks in his heart, so is he."[1] Therefore, your thoughts reveal who you are, and consequently, affect what you become and what you achieve. Jesus said that all things are possible to a person who believes.[2] The question is, are you making room for all that is possible in your life?

If they can do it...

I read a story of a ninety-eight-year-old man who showed up at the Empire State Building to run the stairs at the annual Run Up. Someone asked, "Sir, why are you here? You're too old. It isn't possible for you to run those stairs!" But the old man was adamant about running them.

Can you imagine how he looked? He didn't look the same as the twenty-year-olds in their Nike shorts and Nike shoes!

Someone else asked, "Sir, why do you want to run those stairs so badly? People in their forties don't do it. Most people in their thirties don't even do it."

He said, "Because I need to get ready to run the Boston Marathon."

He was determined to run because he thought it was possible. That ninety-eight-year-old ran up the stairs all the way to the top, and he ran all the way back down, even beating some of the twenty- and thirty-year-olds.[3]

I wonder, what is possible for you?

A forty-year-old nun named Madonna who had never exercised or taken care of her body a day of her life decided, "I need to start doing something with my body, or my body is going to start doing something with me on a bigger scale." (We've all been there.)

She said, "I'm going to start by walking a block." So the first day she walked a block. The next day she walked two, and the next day she walked three. Over the next thirty-three years, she ran more than 330 marathons and 32 Ironman competitions of swimming, biking, and marathon running. Somewhere in her mind, she made room for what was possible.[4]

Be ignorant of your impossibilities.

Think big

Your future is what you envision it to be. What you see is what you gravitate toward, and what gets your attention always captures your affection. What's capturing your attention and your affection right now?

Walt Disney went from creating a mouse to creating Disneyland to creating Disney World. The Wright brothers thought it would be cool to get off the ground, so they developed an airplane. Thomas Edison had an idea about developing the light bulb. Abraham Lincoln had a dream, too. He envisioned making it to the White House, and although he had many setbacks, his dream never dissipated; he always thought it was possible, and he arrived there.

On a normal Friday at the Galilean shore, a fisherman named Simon was knocking back beers and shooting darts with his buddies when his brother walked in and said, "Hey, God the Messiah is on this planet and he wants to talk to you."

Startled at first, Simon brushed it off. But his little brother persisted. "You need to come. He told me he wants to talk to you right now."

So Simon went with his brother to Jesus, and I love what Jesus said when he looked at him. "I know they call you Simon (which means someone who is wayward, someone who fluctuates), but I'll call you powerful." With that, Jesus changed Simon's name to Peter.

God always speaks to your potential—to what can be—rather than to your limitation.

He's always leaning into you, making demands on you. That's what you may be feeling right now—a new demand on your life that causes you not to stay where you are. Destinations, sensations, and creations are waiting for you. Tap into the big thoughts residing on the inside!

Deep-end living

A year and a half after the initial conversation between Jesus and Peter, Jesus showed up at Peter's workplace, at the shore where he fished. It was daytime and Peter had just finished fishing all night because that was the natural time to fish.

Jesus arrived with hundreds of people. How would you like it if Jesus showed up at your business with that many people?

Jesus said, "Hey, I need your boat so I can talk to all these people without getting crushed." But Jesus noticed something very significant—Peter's boat was anchored in shallow water.

Does that sound familiar? Your life has been anchored in the shallow, the insignificant, the unprofound. Shallow is safe because you can touch bottom. It's a place where no risk is involved, where you blend in, and where you stay even though you know it reduces who you are and doesn't serve where you are going. You sense you were created for more, but you'd rather play it safe at a job that doesn't fit and serve the real you with your gift and abilities. When you see a need, you stay safe in the shallow end of giving, hoarding your resources rather than giving them because you're afraid to lose something.

So what does Jesus say to them (and to you and me)? Launch out into the deep!

When Jesus said to launch out into the deep, Peter responded, "I've toiled all night, I'm tired, and I've caught nothing." In America, we've become so addicted to a life without dreams, so addicted to a life of I'm tired, I'm over-worked, I'm overwhelmed, and I'm empty-handed; I don't have time to dream, and I don't have time to think.

Life can hit you that way in your mind. You find yourself in a state of hope that's been *deferred* rather than where hope has made you *determined*.

Your enemy, the devil, battles for your mind because he knows if he can defeat you in your mind, he will defeat you in your experience. He will keep you anchored in the shallow end. Nothing is more frustrating than trying to swim in shallow water!

What if God personally walked out of the pages of this book at this moment and introduced himself to you? What if he said, "Right now, I'd like to give you much more than you've ever believed possible, but your imagination will restrict how much I can give to you. Will you allow me to launch you into life's deep end? Are you willing to get in over your head with me?"

Something deeper, something bigger, something better

God's plan is for you to experience a greater marriage, a greater dimension of finances, a greater degree of health; it's his plan for you to keep increasing and for your journey in life to keep getting brighter and brighter.

Have you dwelt in the land of okay long enough? How are you? Oh, I'm okay. How are your relationships? Oh, they're okay. How are your financials? They're okay. Has "I'm okay" become the theme of your life? Your potential never takes shape until demands are placed on your thinking. God is a good father, stirring up what is possible in your mind so that you find your potential.

God gets more glory out of your success than your failure.

God is the God of supernatural interventions. He gets us out of things and into new things—new jobs, new relationships, and new opportunities to go places we've never gone before. God wants to take you to new capacities. He didn't put you on this planet to barely get by, to be status quo, or to blend in. No, God gets more glory out of your success than your failure. He likes it when his kids shine brightly on the planet—if they don't, it looks bad on his resume. But the extent of his activity and ability in your life are determined by the way you think and what you make room for him to do.

Risk taker, Caretaker, or Undertaker?

What are you choosing to be—a risk taker, a caretaker, or an undertaker?

An *undertaker* criticizes people for having an imagination and acting on it.

A *caretaker* is one who plays it safe and lives in the realm of "I am comfortable, I can stand, I can touch." A caretaker is like a snorkeler, staying in only five to ten feet of water where he can see the small fish. That's cool, but a scuba diver can go down to one thousand feet and see some big fish! The question is, will you allow *the little* to stop your desire and your dream for seeing *the big?* What you think is possible is all in your imagination.

Risk takers are willing to say, "I have one chance at life. I have one chance in this moment, and I am going to dream out loud for the whole world to hear."

Your imagination is your preview of the coming attractions in your life.

Catching the vision

What are you seeing in your future? Without a vision, you perish; you go out of bounds, you do dumb stuff like the person who becomes an addict or the person who has an affair. Their actions don't mean they're horrible people, but that they've lost sight of where they're going in life.

Where are you going? What are you reaching for?

You must ask yourself, is the vision for my life being inspired from myself or inspired from God? A vision inspired from you focuses on what you can get, and a vision from God always focuses on what you can give.

Have others suggested you have to think or act in a way that violates your vision? Let this be a moment where you decide to color outside the lines. If you never reach outside the boundaries drawn by the expectations of others, you will always produce what has already been done. If you don't have a vision and a plan for your own life, you'll find it easy to get swallowed up in somebody else's vision.

God is always multidimensional, always progressive. That's why he says, "Listen, it's time to enlarge your boundaries."[5] It's time to go beyond the barricades and bad breaks of your life. You get to set the boundaries of your life that will either expand or shrink your life.

Are you living as a mini version of yourself? Living like that reminds me of the character of Mini Me in the Austin Powers' movies. Your *me* has shrunk because your expectations have been cramped and stifled by people saying you can't expect *that* when the economy is so bad, you can't go *there* with your lack of education. Who said? Not everyone will understand the dreamer inside you, but without a dream, what do you have? From this point on, refuse to allow other people's thoughts and attitudes to condemn you to a life of mediocrity and frustration.

Helen Keller, a woman born without sight and hearing, has been quoted many times as saying, "The only thing worse than being born blind is having sight but no vision."

This is a powerful truth for you and me to embrace. The power of vision cannot be overstated, for your vision is your future. Start making room for your vision—you must conceive it on the inside before you see it on the outside. See yourself rising to new levels of success; enjoying a healthier body, increased finances, and happier relationships. Forget the past and press ahead. Don't let negative voices dull your enthusiasm; you know the ones—they say you can only go as far as your parents have gone. Break through the ceiling. God has designed you to go further!

Your vision is your future.

If you've accomplished all that you've planned for yourself, you haven't planned enough. Raise your level of expectation so you don't settle for a small life and a limited view of what can happen in your future.

You are made in the image of God, to think and act like him. God thinks increase and more than enough. He wants to outdo what's he's already accomplished in your life, so make room for more in your thinking.

You will get what you expect out of life. Thomas Jefferson said, "I like dreams of the future better than I like the history of my past."

It's time to make room for God in your mind and unpack your dream for what is possible.

Destiny or habit?

At the Starbucks near my house, the employees know me well and for a long period of time they would always say, "Rex, would you like the usual" until one day, I ordered something different. Change is good. It reorders your mind and opens up new possibilities.

Are you tired of ordering the usual off the menu? Is what you're doing now working for you? There's more to you than meets the eye; more that needs expression through your imagination!

Will this be the day you use your imagination and say, "I'm going to try something different? Maybe I would enjoy this, maybe I would enjoy going for more walks, maybe I would enjoy a better lifestyle in a healthy body. Maybe I would enjoy my relationships more if I look at what I can give rather than what I can get. Maybe I would enjoy my vacations more if I went somewhere else and didn't take my cell phone. Maybe I would enjoy eating in restaurants better if I went an hour outside of my community to eat. I wonder what could happen?" Go ahead and wonder...

God birthed you so you could enjoy your life, not just go through the routine.

Far too many of us have agreed with things that don't require us to use our imagination for what can be. We have agreed to a life without dreams. We have agreed to what is present, not what could be in the future. We have agreed to live within the limits of other people's opinions and expectations, but those are cramping our style, hindering our abilities, our talents, and our relationships.

Move toward the new

Learn from the past, but don't stay there. It's time to make the old ceiling your new floor. It's time to reach where no one has gone before. Don't replay history, don't repeat the past. It's time not to have a rerun, but a new season in your life.

God says don't remember the old things![6] Ask him what he's up to. He wants to tell you. When he designed you, he put dreams and destination inside you and planned for incredible things to come out of you. The Bible discloses that if you can't see what God is doing, you stumble all over yourself; but when you do what he reveals, then you're blessed.

All breakthroughs begin with a change of belief. Why don't you ask God what he has for you next? Surely he would let you in on some secrets. Surely he would let you in on them because he wants you to arrive there. When you arrive, you're going to help somebody. You're going to change somebody and you're going to enjoy a greater life.

It's time to take the limits off. When a person puts a limit on what he can do, he puts a limit on what he will do and what God can do. God is a big God; check out his resume:

He created a world when there wasn't one.

He parted the Red Sea through Moses who was a murderer.

He birthed the Messiah through a young woman named Mary.

He spoke through Peter who chopped off a man's ear and denied knowing Jesus.

The Bible says, "Is the Spirit of the Lord restricted?"[7] The Spirit of God is only restricted, confined, and limited by your imagination of what can be. By changing your thinking and beliefs, you change what is possible in your life.

Belief systems

Believe today so you can become tomorrow.

Our beliefs always tell us what is possible and what is not, who we can become and who we can't. Let me ask you, are your beliefs helping you or hindering you? Become who you want to become.

Are you saying, "What if it doesn't work out?"

I'm saying, "What if it does?"

We become so conditioned to pessimistic thoughts such as, this relationship will probably turn out like the last one and this business venture will probably fail because of the struggling economy, that we begin our day dreading the worst instead of expecting the best.

Before you get out of bed in the morning, do you lie there thinking of a million things that could go wrong that day? Thoughts like these:

I have to drive to work. It's going to take a long time because traffic is going to be bad. Then I have to deal with my boss who's grumpy in the mornings. After that, I have to go home and help the kids do their homework. Then I have to mow the lawn. I'm going to have to do what my wife asks me to do. When am I ever going to get some time to myself? When can I do what *I* want to do?

You're not even getting a chance to imagine what can be because you're locked in a form of fear called dread. It's time to change.

How about starting your day imagining more joy, better relationships, more peace? Look at life wide open by faith of what can be.

Pessimism, idealism, and realism

A pessimist sees through the negative lenses of disappointment and thinks, people have let me down, so why try again? But it takes faith to stay in God's progressive movement. It takes faith to stay current with God.

How about starting your day imagining more joy, better relationships, more peace?

An idealist lives with the "someday syndrome." This person thinks, someday, everything will fall into place—my dreams will come true, my body will be healthy, and my relationships will be full of passion and purpose without any effort on my part because God will do it all for me.

A realist sees what is but closes the gap through a determination to take action.

See it to be it

One night as I was speaking, I looked out across the seated crowd and saw a very muscular man. Afterward, I approached him and noticed he was over six feet tall with a deep voice. He looked at me and said, "You fire me up, Rex Crain. You stir me up."

Recognizing him as Ken Norton, the former heavyweight champion known for knocking out Muhammad Ali and cracking his jaw in half, I said, "Why did you come tonight?"

He said, "I'm in pain because of some physical challenges, Rex Crain, and I need to get better." So I prayed for him and God touched him physically in a very special way, where his pain was visibly alleviated.

Then I asked him, "What did it take for you to defeat Muhammad Ali, who was known as the greatest boxing champion ever?"

He said, *"Rex Crain, I had to see it. You got to see it to be it.* What you don't see, you can't have. I had to train and condition my mind just like I trained and conditioned my body. If I never fed my mind, then all I would have is my body. I had to see it so I could be it. You got to see it to be it, Rex Crain."

See it to have it

Christians, Jews, and Muslims alike all honor a man who lived thousands of years ago. He is known as the father of faith and the friend of God. His name is Abraham. Years ago, the creator of the universe came to his friend to give him an amazing word and message.

It all started when Abraham heard the voice of an unseen person calling to him. It was God saying, "I want you to come out of your tent. Come out and count the number of stars that light up the sky. I'm looking for someone to dream with."

Abraham said, "God, right now? Sarah just got a new, sexy outfit from Victoria's Secret today and I'm about to get lucky, God. She's making chocolate chip cookies and we're watching *Jerusalem Idol,* so this isn't going to work tonight, God. Come back tomorrow."

God said in a whisper, "Abraham. I need you to come out of your tent. I need someone to dream with. I have something to impart to you."

"God, for real, can we do this tomorrow?"

"No, I need to talk to you tonight. There's a message in the stars waiting for you."

So Abraham told his wife, "I'll be back. Don't change your mind. Stay in the mood."

In this story, God called Abraham *out of his tent*. The tent represents the limited place of our thinking. Our potential is limited by our thoughts.

Everybody comes with "potential capacity"—goods, power, potency, promise, talent—and how much we use is determined by the limitations of our thinking.

You don't have to live by the limitations of your logic when you can live out of the inspiration of your imagination.

So, God called Abraham out and said, "I want you to lie on your back and look at the stars. There is a message in the stars, Abraham. Count them with me and imagine."

Now, Abraham didn't have nice grass to lie down on. The ground was dirty, rocky, and covered with animal droppings so it wasn't comfortable or convenient for him. You might not be

You might not be comfortable when you begin to dream and imagine the world you want to live in, but if you don't imagine, you're going to stay frustrated.

comfortable when you begin to dream and imagine the world you want to live in, but if you don't imagine, you're going to stay frustrated.

It's time to dream again! It's time to be awakened and aware and active in a dream that's inside you once again.

God said to Abraham, "I want you to look up at the stars and count."

So Abraham started out, speaking to himself and God, "One, two, three, four, five, six...thirty-two, thirty-three...sixty-one...ah, there are too many to count; it's limitless! This is cramping my mind. I can't handle this!"

"Abraham, lie back down again and stop complaining. I want you to count the stars again."

Perplexed, Abraham attempted to mentally wrap his mind around what the Man upstairs was up to in asking him to count the limitless expanse of the stars. He decided to continue his quest to follow the message of the unseen God's voice until God explained that the number of stars Abraham saw would be a sign of the number of his descendants to come.[8] At this stage of Abraham's life, he was successful, married, and financially well off. Yet, in God's eyes, he hadn't even begun to tap into the main events God had planned for his life.

You, too, may have thought that you've reached your limits and gone as far as you can go. Yet, just like Abraham, the voice of the unseen person is calling you out of your comfortable tent to align yourself with the stars so you can access the rest of your untold story.

"One, two, three, four, five, six, seven...nine hundred, nine hundred twenty-one...God, it's too much. I forgot where I was."

"Abraham, that's the way your life is about to become; everything you can see, you can have. Now part ways with people and things that don't serve your imagination of where you want to go, and after that, everywhere you can see, you can have. What you see, you can have."[9]

What can you see?

All vision creates sensation and what fascinates you becomes fastened to you, so imagine what you want and what it would feel like to have it.

Action thoughts:

Where could my gift and abilities thrive? How could my relationships improve? What would I do if I had more energy and more money?

Go ahead—dream about what you envision for your life. *Imagine what can be.*

$\mathcal{3}$

Destiny Powers

It was a typical day for Mother Teresa. For over twenty years, she had taught wealthy children in India. Every day, she had ignored the suffering poor in the slums nearby. God had placed within her a strong gift of mercy, but she hadn't discovered it yet.

Walking home one night, she heard a woman cry out for help. She turned, and discovered a woman in severe physical suffering, near the point of death. Mother Teresa picked her up and carried her to a hospital, but the hospital refused to treat a poor woman.

Frantically, Mother Teresa took her to another hospital, where the same event unfolded. In the absence of medical treatment, Mother Teresa took the woman home. Later that night, the woman died in her arms.

In that moment, Mother Teresa decided not to allow this to happen to another person within her sphere of influence. She decided to give her life to ease the pain of suffering people and to fight for them to have the love, dignity, and value God placed upon their lives.[1]

After her gift of mercy awoke, Mother Teresa became such a strong advocate for the poor that she became a household name around the world.

Everybody is born with slumbering destiny powers. When God made you in his image, he put something intricate, something wonderful inside of you; he gave you a gift to benefit the world around you. No one else on this planet can do what you can do, the way you can do it. You offer a gift to society that no one else brings; if you don't bring it, it won't be brought!

Oliver Wendell Holmes Jr. writes, "What lies behind us and what lies before us are tiny matters compared to what lies within us." Albert Einstein wrote, "Everybody is a genius." So I ask you, what is your genius?

Discovering your gift

A great way to recognize your gift is to identify the skills that create passion inside you.

What slumbering destiny powers lie within you? What goes unrecognized will go unrewarded. I want you to live rewarded for the destiny powers you carry.

It will help you to ask yourself, what gift, talent, or abilities dominate my thoughts? Your passions may be obvious to you, or maybe you've never discovered them because of the busyness of life and other people's ideas about you.

A great way to recognize your gift is to identify the skills that create passion inside you. I remember being in New York at a John Legend concert. With about sixty other people, I had the privilege of watching him rehearse before the concert started. As he began to play the piano and sing, his passion for music filled the atmosphere and instantly captivated us. His passion embraced us, transcending time.

Do you remember doing something and thinking, oh my goodness, that was one of the most amazing moments of my life—I loved the feeling I got from doing that! Your gift will leave clues in the skill that leaves a memory you want to come back to.

Do you think about singing? Serving people? Speaking? Fixing things? Encouraging? Do you have an unrelenting desire to educate and empower people with knowledge in a specific field? Inventive ideas that improve lives may be what keep you up late at night. Closing business deals may be your specialty. Maybe showing mercy to the hurting and homeless is one of the dominant forces that makes you feel alive.

If all your bills were paid forever, what would you love enough to give your life to? What you would do if fear, failure, and money were no object? Where would you invest your time?

Your answer is a clue to your gift. Your gift is a clue to what God has assigned you to do. Walt Disney said, "First find something you like to do so much you'd gladly do it for nothing; then learn to do it so well people are happy to pay you for it."

For me, the answer is to help you live an intentional life. I have to help you become deliberate about the gift you've been given so you commit to forming a reality around it.

Whatever gift and talents you think about most reveals the destiny powers alive inside you. Your passion and potential lie within those destiny powers.

Developing your gift

Is your life filled with passion and purpose, or does it seem uneventful and uninspiring?

If you lack passion, could it be you've never developed and built a reality around the destiny powers within? The very existence of those abilities is proof you have a responsibility to develop them. Your gift is evidence God knows the earth needs the unimaginable potential he placed inside of you. He wants you to discover and develop the unique set of abilities and talents he gave you, for in them lies the passion, potency, and pleasure through which you can experience a rich and rewarded life.

I feel sad knowing that many wonderful and capable people live unrewarded for the potential that lies inside them. Their lives have become trapped by lifestyle choices that don't allow their rich power, creativity, and unused success to come forth. The release of their potential would offer them the enjoyment and fulfillment their spirit craves.

Potential is released when we place a demand on our gift.

Imagine what the world would lose if you were never to discover and develop your potential. Would the world miss out on a work of art, a solution to a problem, or a cure for a disease? Whatever it is, make the decision not to rob yourself or the world around you another day of the rich resources lying within you.

If you fail to give responsibility to your gift and abilities, then the next generation will enter the museum of life and see a vacant spot where your gift's contribution to society is missing. I don't want them to see a vacant spot; I want them to see that you were responsible with what you were given, that you were willing to count the personal cost, and that you sacrificed to give your best.

You don't have to do all things well; you weren't created to do all things and be all things. God wants you in place in your sphere of influence to honor his name and become a light. That comes by using what you have. Don't let it stagnate another day. Refuse to dabble with your gift.

Scripts, books, and businesses are waiting to exist. Give yourself to what you have; in fact, thrust yourself into your studies, or into running a company, or into writing music.

My friend, Dr. Myles Munroe, writes, "The greatest tragedy in your life will not be your death, but what dies with you at death."[2]

Don't let your gift die with you. Make the world a better place.

The Bible says everybody has a gift and Matthew 25 talks about using it. Some people make an investment; some people make an excuse, but a gift is God's ingredient to give a life of success, a life of growth and expansion.

Success is not a destination; success is continual growth, development, and expansion of skills.

You have to work at your gift, talents, and skills for them to work in you.

Are you continually cultivating your destiny powers? You have to work at your gift, talents, and skills for them to work in you. God says his power is at work in you, but are you working the power?

Theodore Roosevelt said, "Your ability needs responsibility to expose its possibilities. Do what you can with what you have where you are."

People who excel and exceed limits and become a blessing to mankind are people who believe they have ability to accomplish something that has never been done. To do so, they must give that ability a responsibility that could change the world. That's when miracles happen.

Off the sidelines

For you to live life intentionally from this point forward, you must become purposeful about your God-given gift and abilities. When you become intentional about your destiny powers, you become determined to act and live in a signature way—a way that leaves a profound effect.

Most people around us have made the passive choice to live an uneventful and fruitless life by embracing a life marked by self-comfort and convenience. Their destiny powers go untapped and unexplored, which ultimately leaves them with an unprofound life. They abort their gift. An abortion is really self-comfort at the expense of fruitfulness. A lot of people opt for comfort rather than for a fruitful life because they don't want to take responsibility to develop their gift's potential.

As a society, we've become spectators; addicted to watching other people use their abilities to serve the world and improve the quality of their own lives. Yet, while we watch and observe them, we constantly feel a personal dissatisfaction about what we're doing with our own lives and abilities. While we watch other people use what they've been given, we tend to consider our gift as insignificant.

Never despise what you have. When you and I begin to think our gift and abilities are too small and insignificant to explore, we diminish their influence on where they can take us and what we can accomplish or achieve through them, and we start to short-circuit the power and passion in our lives. We limit our lives.

A limited life is a compromised life because we refuse to operate out of the grace that has been given to us to expand and grow. It's nice when people say they believe in the gift within us, but their belief won't make our gift operate. What we need to do is begin to do something with what we have.

The biblical story of the widow with the little bit of oil demonstrated how she never saw an increase in her oil until she used what she had.[3] There is never multiplication or increase in God's realm until a person uses what they have, so when we refuse to use what we have, we lead ourselves into a life of frustration.

If you neglect your gift, you'll live a frustrated life. Living a frustrated life is watching other people succeed while you go nowhere fast. Be responsible and own what you have. If you don't do something with what you have, you'll never grow. You'll stay in that same place.

You might say, "Well, conditions aren't right. I'm overwhelmed by things right now." Well, the worst thing you can do is stay in isolation, all by yourself. The best thing you can do is go through recovery and discovery at the same time. The more you give yourself to discovery, the more your recovery will speed up. When you begin to use what you have, you create a momentum for reaching forward, rather than for reaching back. Because of the gift God put inside you, you have the ability to go forward and have true success.

Start somewhere

I remember when nobody listened to my speeches; back when I'd speak to the empty seats in my grandpa's church. That's when I began using my gift right where I was. Are you thinking, I don't know where to begin? Begin somewhere.

Begin at your local church, the Y, or your Boys & Girls Clubs. Begin using what you have right now in places where you can serve. What do you have in your hand that you can use immediately? Will you begin to write a poem? Begin to work in a children's department at a church? Begin to volunteer at a hospital? As you serve, maybe you'll stumble upon a gift such as the mercy gift Mother Teresa had.

People want to be paid for their gift right off the bat, but that's the wrong motive. Instead, focus on the wealth within. When you invest in the gift within by developing your abilities, talents, and skills, payment will follow.

Nimrod was a man who lived back in the early days of biblical history. The Bible shows that Nimrod had aspirations that could not rest. Does that sound like you? Do your aspirations and dreams and abilities shout even when you're silent? "He was a mighty hunter before the Lord" (Gen. 10:9 KJV). The Bible says he began to give himself to his craft, and that tells me something: he had a moment when he realized there was more to him than showed at the moment.[4] He became very diligent at becoming a great hunter, to the point where his influence expanded over several cities in different regions. Unfortunately, he used it against God with the building of the Tower of Babel. His passion wasn't driven by God's purpose; therefore, it brought pain.[5]

Shaping and stirring

Your potential is always wrapped up in your abilities and skills. Your skills can be sharp or dull; they can be stirred up or left stagnant.

I've spent a lot of time in my life imagining what my gift could do, and now, I've spoken in a lot of places that I used to dream about speaking in. I used to intentionally put myself in environments that stirred up my gift. I would go to hear speakers at the top of their game and entertainers who were known to move and rock a crowd, so I could feel my gift come alive; this would awaken the passion within me and allow me to dream about what the gift in my life could accomplish.

Even though people used to tell me I wasn't cut out to be a speaker, I knew that a speaking gift was real in my life. I put definition to it and shaped it by watching professionals at their craft. They were models that motivated me to say, "Man, I can do that."

Maybe someone has motivated you to think, I would love to do that! That doesn't mean you have to leave your job right now, but you can begin to work on that passion, that gift and skill, and it won't be long before they will create space and opportunity for expansion. You'll outgrow where you are financially and relationally. You'll live by the purpose of God.

Get off your assets

Perhaps you've been wasting your gift and skills because you're blind to their potency. Sitting on your assets has

Someone on this planet needs and is waiting for the release and the reward your gift will bring to them.

prevented you from taking radical action to create a radical result.

Someone on this planet needs and is waiting for the release and the reward your gift will bring to them. If you fail to use your gift, you will live out of an unresourceful, unrecognized, and unsatisfied state. The opportunity to live in a resourceful and satisfied state is identifying and activating the gift that is alive in you.

From dark to light

By the age of eleven, Stevie Wonder had already demonstrated a gift for music; he could sing and play the harmonica, piano, and drums. The more instruments he mastered, the more he was prepared to master. Blindness didn't hinder his expansion.

Sometimes you have to prepare in the dark before you see the result in the light. You have to talk about it and think about what it can do. You have to make plans, and you have to begin to use the very gift itself. Desire without diligence leads to illusion.

A lot of people are living stagnant, disillusioned lives because they hope in something without putting any effort into it. The only way you become good at something is with effort. I became a professional baseball player, not just because I was skilled and gifted, but because I worked hard at it.

Skill always comes in the form of a seed, but if the seed never grows, then it never becomes. The potential is in the seed, but it must reproduce. We plant the seed through our actions, thoughts, preparation, and planning. I can't have a harvest without planting seed, so I have to plant the seed of my resources—my time, energy, and money—into things that will grow and develop.

Coach John Wooden said, "If I fail to prepare, I am preparing to fail."

Are you preparing for more?

Are you an encourager? Then encourage people until you're blue in the face. As you do, your gift will cause your influence to expand. If your gift is the ability to sing, then if I were you, I would sing and practice and begin developing a relationship with somebody that sings better than I do. I would get involved where everyone sees my gift. The more you sing, the more opportunities to sing God will bring. You might want all the opportunities to just show up, but that's not the way it works. What you develop in the dark, God rewards in the light.

Kryptonite that weakens

Kryptonite weakened Superman and his superpowers. It reduced him from a superhero to a common man. What weakens your destiny powers?

Some people fear success, and others fear failure. Sometimes fear is more than an emotion; sometimes fear is a spirit sent to harass, torment, and prevent you from stepping out. Fear wants you to focus on your past disappointments and wants you to worry about failing in the future.

Fear wants to remove you from moving.

Fear wants to remove you from moving. It wants to paralyze you and your potential. The enemy knows when you move in your gift, others will receive a benefit and value. He doesn't want that to happen because (1) someone else's life will change, and (2) your life will grow, resulting in excitement about helping someone again.

I can't tell you how much my own spirit soars and grows every time I use what I have. Every time, I want to go to a higher level and see my gift and skill develop even more because I realize the benefit in touching people.

I love speaking. My love for it drives me to be better at it, so I work on my craft. I cultivate it, care for it, define and refine it. I fight for it.

Any time you start using your gift and changing people's lives, obstacles like fear will want to hinder it. So care for it; protect it against people and powers that want to defeat it.

Call to action

How will you begin now, right where you are? What is one step you can take to use or refine your gift?

Inspiration without action is useless. A small change will create a big difference. It's time to identify your gift and activate your genius.

Your significance is not in your similarity to others, but in your difference.

4

Self Gone Missing

What if you lost the most valuable thing in your life? What would that be?

What if you lost yourself? For countless millions, this has become a reality. Through busy lifestyles, difficult relationships, and endless routines we can't locate ourselves. The most pivotal questions—who am I? why am I here? what is my life supposed to be about?—can leave us feeling empty inside because we sense something is missing.

I remember a time as a teenager when I decided to move away from Orlando back to California where I had grown up. It was a big move for me because I was feeling the need to do something fresh and new, but like most young people, I didn't know what that was.

My dad had flown in from California to drive across America with me. This was to be about a four-day journey, just Dad and me.

We made sure everything was packed just right, and that all my accounts were taken care of at the Florida banks. I had decided to empty my accounts, converting the money into a single check and a couple thousand in cash. I kept them in my wallet, confident I had the ability to protect them till I could get to a bank in California.

Our trip started amazingly well—great conversation filled the car as we talked about life and growing up. We decided early that if we made it to Texas, we would find a hotel to rest for the night and begin our journey the following morning. After dinner, we made one last stop to get some gas, and then we felt like we could drive another hour or two, so we kept driving. Finally, we came to a hotel off Highway 10. Tired from our long driving expedition, we looked forward to rest.

As I went to pay the hotel clerk, I became aware that something was wrong. My wallet containing my ID card along with the check and all my cash were nowhere to be found! As panic raced through me, I went on a deliberate search for my wallet.

In a nervous frenzy, my dad and I emptied and filled, and emptied and filled the car four times. As one search after the other kept coming up empty, a horrible feeling of loss grew in the pit of my stomach.

I remember sitting there crying, at a loss for words. My dad comforted me the best he could, saying, "Let's return to the gas station. Maybe you laid it down somewhere."

We made it back in record time. We got out of the car and searched the bathroom, the bushes, and even the car twice more. As the search kept coming up empty, the idea struck me that I would never recover my money and ID. Maybe someone had stolen them, or maybe I had just misplaced them.

As we drove to the nearest hotel, I began to cry in despair. I asked God to somehow and in some way restore my identity and valuables. As we pulled into La Quinta hotel, I turned around to grab some clothes out of my bag in the backseat. To my amazement, sitting on top of the bag in plain sight, was my wallet! I found all of my cash sitting inside, folded all nice and neat. A sense of wonder filled my heart! What was lost was now supernaturally restored.

Like me, maybe you've lost something. Maybe you've lost your wallet, keys, wedding ring, or worse, your sense of self. If so, there's good news...

You are what you think

Your self-image is the picture you carry of yourself. It's who you see yourself to be.

How you see yourself has a massive effect on your success and the quality of your relationships. It will affect how far you go in life, and whether or not you fulfill your destiny.

The reason your self-concept is so important is because you will think, act, and respond as the person you think you are. Psychologists have proven that you will consistently act and behave in a manner that is in harmony with the image you carry of yourself. It determines how big or how small

How you see yourself has a massive effect on your success and the quality of your relationships.

your life becomes. It will, from this moment on, determine whether you're a giver or a taker, a lover or a fighter, powerful or pitiful.

If what you see when you look in the mirror is a failure, you're setting yourself up to fail. If you see yourself as dull, you will live without luster, constantly attracting dull people to your life. If, on the other hand, you see yourself as powerful, you will attract powerful people and greater opportunities to your life. Countless wonderful people see themselves as victims. They feel defeated and depressed, and their lives are characterized by feeling sorry for themselves. If you constantly see yourself as barely making it—always having problems, never happy—you will unconsciously move down a path that sabotages you from the start of every relationship and project. My goal, as your friend, is to stop this sick cycle from continuing. It begins with changing the way you see yourself.

Your self-image has a huge impact on what you receive from God and others, because what you receive is a direct result of what you believe.

Your self-image is the prophet to your future. If you see inaccurately, your life will suffer and you will constantly be plagued with insecurity and inferiority that will leave you powerless and joyless.

I have discovered that for my life to improve, my self-image has to improve. This is because I never rise higher than the image I see of myself. It affects how I feel, and how I feel is the result of what I'm thinking about myself.

Your fate lies in the way you view yourself.

Call to action

I believe the rest of your life can be the best of your life, no matter where you've been and what you've been through, and it starts by making these statements:

Who I become and what I experience in my life from here on out is directly related to who I think I am and believe I am. How I view myself will be the determining factor of the success and prosperity of my life. The release of my potential will never be able to extend beyond the way I see myself.

The man in the mirror

Michael Jackson sang, "I'm starting with the man in the mirror." The question is, who do you see when you look in the mirror? Do you like what you see?

I remember the joy and pain of being thirteen. What an awkward place to be! I woke up one day to the vision of two rather large spots on my face. This was something I had never experienced before—pimples. This was not the greatest thing that could have happened to a young guy who was going through the experience of puberty, trying to feel good about himself in relation to the opposite sex.

As I showed my mom my two pimples, instead of finding some comfort and relief, she became nervous and said we needed to go to the dermatologist. I reassured her it was only two pimples and we should just try to use Clearasil or Oxy, yet she persisted in taking me to the doctor.

As the doctor and nurse were finishing up with me, they gave me a cream they said would clear up the pimples. What they failed to tell me was that this cream would burn my face bright red and that I would see myself for years to come as the person with the red face.

I became aware of how red it was when I returned to school and people kept asking why my face was so red. Then I began to hear them calling me "red face." On the outside, I did my best to act like it didn't bother me, but on the inside, I began to think that something was wrong with me. I began to feel I didn't measure up to the others. In my own mind, I began to feel inferior to others around me, which lowered my confidence in myself.

Who do you see when you look in the mirror? Has your self gone missing?

I tried to cover it up with my grandma's makeup, trying any remedy that made any promise to remove my insecurity. I wasn't comfortable with the person I saw in the mirror.

Who do you see when you look in the mirror? Has your self gone missing?

Labels

Your view of yourself is shaped by what you see and hear.

See: what my surroundings communicate, what society shows me

Hear: people's comments and labels

Labels are words people say to us that are out to describe who we are, what we possess, and how far we can go. From our earliest years, it seems like people and parents and peers are all out to define us. Some of these definitions cripple our potential and limit what we attempt to do or want to pursue.

Before the world ever attempted to describe and define your life, God created you without all their input. He designed a person he approves of, who has significance and eternal meaning to him.

Action thought:

Statistics reveal that most people only use about 10 percent of their brains. Why then, would I allow 10 percent (on a good day) of someone's brain to determine who I really am?

Don't allow anyone's opinion, even yours, to be bigger than God's.

Girl gone missing

From talking to others, I've discovered we like to portray a persona that doesn't line up with the real image we see of ourselves.

I experienced this firsthand as I ate lunch with a couple of TV producers and a girl on a reality show that was making lots of headlines. She was known for being the bad girl. Acting provocative and racy was her mechanism for keeping everybody intrigued with her. Yet, I could see the girl behind the persona, so I asked her, "Have you ever wanted people to see the real you? Do you ever desire for people to see more than they've seen on TV?" She leaned toward me from across the table, and her countenance changed into that of a little girl, waiting to be told something wonderful about herself. I said, "There is more to you than meets the eye. Inside you, there is a heart, love, ability, and creativity the world has never seen." As I spoke those affirming words, her eyes filled with tears. For the first time in a long time, or maybe even ever, she sensed her real self.

Who was she? Simply a girl who went missing. No, her picture wasn't on the back of a milk carton. She was a girl who had known abuse from an early age that left her ignorant about who she was and why she was here. That's why she lived like many of us, wondering and wandering from place to place, coping with an existence that was less than it was designed to be. All because she saw herself through limiting lenses.

Call to action

Take a look at your lenses.

When you look in the mirror, do you see somebody who is rich or poor? Healthy or sick? Do you see someone who is lovable and attractive, or someone who is unlovable and doesn't measure up?

The thoughts and feelings you have about yourself will determine what you'll reach for in life. "It's not who you are that holds you back; it's who you think you're not" (John Maxwell).[1]

Design or default?

Many years ago there lived a man by the name of Saul who became Israel's first king. When it was almost time for his coronation, he was nowhere to be found. Where was he? He was out looking for lost asses (or in our day, lost donkeys). Unfortunately, he didn't see himself as a king, so he lived with an ass mentality.

Like Saul, when we see ourselves inaccurately, we chase after what we lost, instead of understanding who we are and then acting out of that knowledge. We live only in recovery, not in discovery, like a cat with gum on its tail running around in circles.

Maybe you feel like you're running around in circles, going nowhere fast, spinning your wheels—only because you're not seeing your value. You're trying to recover something rather than discover who you really are in God.

We can either live by design or by default.

I have learned that we can either live by design or by default. Think of it this way:

Living by design

My spiritual identity is based upon who God, my creator, says I am. His desire is for me to see and esteem myself the way he sees and esteems me. My real self stems from my spiritual identity.

Living by default

1. *My enemy's identity:* The devil is my accuser; therefore, he wants me to see myself through my faults, my flaws, and my failures. He wants me to live in inferiority and shame, living distant and detached from the person I'm called to be. His goal is to blind my eyes so he can maneuver me away from the person God designed me to be.

2. The only other alternative is *my natural identity,* where I see myself based upon my possessions and achievements.

Living by design requires getting my designer's view and intention in inventing me.

God's view

God planned you with infinite value and unlimited potential, and the Bible says that you are fearfully and wonderfully made.[2] It says that God saw you before you were born, and every day of your life was recorded in his book.[3]

And did you know that when God created all of us, he approved of us completely?[4] God might not approve of and love everything we do, but he does approve of who we are designed to be.

Are you second-guessing God's approval because of how you were conceived? It could have been through a one-night stand or even a rape, but the *how* does not defeat the *why*. The fact that you made it here is evidence that your life is necessary.

Your value is not something you have to earn, nor can you earn it. God built it into you when he created you. Psalm 8 says he crowned you with tremendous honor and value.

Jesus came to restore your self gone missing.

You're a work of art, designed for good works, and exclusively chosen to do something magnificent, meaningful, and wonderful.

There is no one like you. Out of seven billion people on this planet, not one of them carries the same fingerprints as you. That alone reveals the value and significance your life holds. God really does approve of you. He sees all the factors, he sees all of your limitations, but he chooses to approve of you and enjoy you. He wants you to feel good about yourself. He knows you're going to make some mistakes, but he's not focusing on your weakness or on what you've done wrong. His focus is on what you do right!

Why wouldn't you buy into an identity like that—one that you receive through the approval of Christ? The alternative is to achieve an identity through your own hard work, and through your own striving.

Refuse to live another day like the distracted king who was looking for what was lost. Instead, embrace the value, the honor, and the dignity God put inside of you.

Action thought:

I will define who I am through God's eyes. To begin to embrace who I am, I will come into agreement with who he says I am. I believe I am lovable, capable, and worthy.

Who are you?

I love to ask people to tell me who they are without telling me what they do. I ask this because so much of our communication about our self-worth and identity is based on who we know and how well we perform. Those things have their place, but I'm more excited about who you are than what you do.

Believe I am lovable, capable, and worthy.

There is more to you than Dad, more to you than a stay-at-home mom, more to you than an actor, more to you than a businessperson, more to you than a student. You are definitely more than your age and weight, more than your past achievements and your bank account.

God designed you and he loves you.

Call to action

Without listing the roles you play and the duties you perform, who are you? What do you love and hate?

Eddie the pothead

On a pleasant Saturday afternoon, I was walking in Hollywood with a friend of mine. We came across a man sitting in a wheelchair and smoking a joint, and we decided to see if he needed anything. We introduced ourselves as Rex and Marshall, and then we simply asked him his name. He gave us an interesting response.

"I am Eddie the pothead."

I laughed at first, then I realized he wasn't laughing, so I asked, "Who told you you're Eddie the pothead?"

"Well, I've always been a screwup and a pothead."

I said, "Surely, there is more to you than that."

"No, I'm just Eddie the pothead."

I said, "God has a better outlook on your life than you just described to me, and he sees you beyond the complex you have of yourself."

We began telling him that he had incredible value, which was why he was still breathing. We told him of the untold worth and unused success that was lying underneath his image of himself.

Because of his wheelchair, I asked him if he was in a lot of pain, and he said he had pain in his back. I asked if I could pray for him, telling him that God and I are friends and that God wanted to liberate his body from physical pain. He asked me if I had special magical powers, and I responded with, "Yeah, something like that."

As we prayed, God began to touch him, and within a minute, he began to rise up out of the wheelchair. He asked, "Where did all the pain go?"

At first I wasn't sure if Jesus healed him or if the pot he was currently smoking made him feel better, but Eddie knew something was different. Something was different because we allowed God's view of him to speak and transform Eddie's life.

I wonder what God's view could restore in your life.

5

Buried Treasure

One night I was in Shamrock Tattoo Shop on Sunset Boulevard with the famous Mark Malone. If you don't know, Mark is a famous tattoo-artist person and a wonderful human being.

That night a friend said, "You've got to go see this guy Mark Malone. I've made it through the six-month waiting list, and tonight, I'm going to get tattooed. He's incredible! He's done influential people from Angelina Jolie to Sean "Diddy" Combs to Biggie Smalls, and Britney Spears, you name them." So I said okay, and we went.

Mark had about six or seven guys doing tattoos in the front of his large shop and it was totally packed, so he took us into the back room. There we saw his assistant Danny doing tattoos and about eight or ten other people.

We were sitting there and I was remembering something about how God has tattoos of us on his hands.[1]

So I said, "Mark, do know that God's got tattoos? The Bible says he has pictures of you on his hands and he can't get his mind off of you. He thinks about you all the time. In fact, he has never thought a bad thought about you."[2]

He said, "No way."

I said, "Let me shock you even more. Jesus has a tattoo on his thigh. It says he's the King of Kings and Lord of Lords. That must mean he created you to be royalty and to dominate, not to be dominated."[3]

And he said, "You're for real, huh?"

I said, "Yeah, I'm not playing."

He said, "Can you give me a Bible?"

I said, "I think we might have one in the car." So Ben, my friend, ran to the car and got my Bible out. He brought the Bible in and he opened it up. Mark stopped doing a tattoo, and he called everybody in the whole tattoo shop together in the back room. Now picture this: people have bottles of alcohol in their hands, they're smoking all kinds of different fragrances out of these things in their fingers, people's body parts are hanging out, and there is loud music playing on Sunset Boulevard. What a wonderful party for God to visit.

Mark said, "I want every one of you to hear this," and they all leaned over me as if I had a *Sports Illustrated* swimsuit issue. I began to tell them that God has tattoos of them on his hands and that Jesus thinks they are royalty and even though they had done crazy stuff, God had never thought a bad thought about them; he created them to dominate, not to be dominated.

And then one of them said, "Jesus was a gangster!"

Well, of course I had to get a tattoo that night. As I was getting a tattoo by Mark's assistant, he said, "Man, this is deep stuff."

I said, "You feel my energy?"

And he said, "Yeah, yeah, I feel your energy."

I said, "Man, that energy has a name and its name is Jesus and he can hook you up to his super. You want to get hooked up?"

He said, "Yeah, my family is struggling, my family is hurting."

I said, "Just act like you're doing my tattoo and don't hurt me. I am going to pray that his energy surges through your body and through your mind and through your family and that it changes things." As I began to pray, the power of God went through that guy's life and through his body. He began to get teary-eyed right there with a *Playboy Magazine* in sight.

Aren't you glad God isn't intimidated by your environment or the label on you? He's more excited about the treasure in you.

Insecurity

How do you see yourself when you're going through something you thought you'd never go through?

I know what it's like to suffer from this kind of insecurity. I went through a hard setback many years ago when someone in my life walked out and said she didn't want to be a part of me anymore. A great deal of my identity was wrapped up in her, so after she left, I didn't enjoy myself. I was broken and feeling abandoned, lost, and rejected. Suffering from insecurity, one minute I was up and the next I was down—meteor-minded, as they say.

LIFE *Lift*

In the Bible, Moses was insecure, too. I call him broken-down Moses because he had all kinds of miracles in his life but he made a bad choice when he killed a man. That choice put him on the back side of the desert where he wandered and wondered how his life would turn out. He was just going through the motions, doing the same old Groundhog Day thing, day in and day out, and feeling like a failure.

"Broken" means "shattered, crushed"[4] and many of us feel that way. We've gone missing due to failures, lustful perversions that people acted out on us as kids, words of angry boyfriends and husbands, and women and even children who have left us feeling less than we are. Like us, Moses was thinking about what could have been, what should have been; wondering who he could have become and how everything was going to turn out in his life.

> *This is what this whole book is about—getting you into the place and the space of isolation, so you will experience revelation.*

One day, God met Moses in the middle of the desert. "Moses, I have a big plan for you."[5]

This is what this whole book is about—getting you into the place and the space of isolation, so you will experience revelation. A revelation and a revolution in your identity will realign you with destiny.

I'm sure Moses was shocked that God would talk to him after he'd killed a man. He probably thought, I wish God hadn't found out about it. I hid the body in the sand, but obviously I didn't hide him well enough. I wonder if his feet were hanging out...God must have seen me running away, wearing my wife beater and my turban. Since then, I've been on the back side of the desert, and I smell like sheep.

God said, "I have a big plan for you. There are a lot of people just like you, Moses, that are suffering. A lot of people that are worse off than you."

"I'm in too much pain. I don't even know who I am anymore. Who am I, God?"

God said, "Instead, let me tell you who *I* am. I am the great I Am, and you are connected with me. Therefore, with everything I Am, I stand behind you."

And that endorsement launched Moses into his destiny.

Maybe you're in a place of thinking, maybe I can just break even. No, that's not good enough. The enemy's goal is to get you to see yourself as weak and ineffective. He wants you to see yourself as broken, because broken-down people break away from their Source. They begin to think about how they can just break even in their lives.

I am helping to unlock you and lift you into the place God has designed for you to appear. Your deliverance always begins with changing your identity, not changing your circumstances. Identifying with Christ allows you to live out of God's ability.

The way to get to the places where God wants you to arrive is to let him breathe his identity into you. Let him breathe into you by agreeing with his thoughts about you.

To do this, maybe you need to do what I did when I felt like a failure years ago. Write a card to yourself about how God sees you and keep it in your back pocket. When I'd feel like a failure, I'd pull mine out and read it out loud: "I am forgiven, I am loved, God is for me not against me, God will never leave me or abandon me, I have the favor of God on my life no matter where I've been and no matter where I've gone. Today is a new day and God's mercies are new every morning. I am more than a conqueror, I am healed, I am growing in grace, and I am growing in strength."

As it did for me, watch how that conversation empowers and uplifts you!

Confidence

Once you get a glimpse of who you are in God's eyes, life becomes fascinating. Even in the midst of failure, even in the midst of flaws, even in the midst of hurt, even in the midst of pain, he begins to breathe his identity into you, changing how you see yourself and how you relate to others. His mercy toward you allows you to be merciful toward yourself and merciful toward others. It's a chain reaction that changes things.

God never created you for failure and frustration but fruitfulness and fullness. The enemy wants to attack your confidence, making you feel guilty. Guilt is a parasite that weakens you, steals your energy, steals your motivation, steals your joy, and steals your confidence to try anything. Guilt says you failed before; it won't work this time.

No, life on your terms is different. This is where you get in the driver's seat and say, "That might have happened then, but that was then and this is now."

But what about the shame you feel? It's time to go back and get another opinion! Let God's opinion make man's opinion irrelevant, including your own. He can do through you what you believe him to do.

Many years ago, there was a man living in survival mode because warring invaders kept plundering and oppressing his country. God chose to appear to him and say, "The Lord is with you, you mighty man of valor!"[6]

It's interesting that God spoke to his potential, not his limitation. His name was Gideon, which meant in Hebrew "a destroyer,"[7] yet he was living a defeated lifestyle, doing business in the caves of Israel so he could hide from his enemies the Midianites. When God appeared to him, he told Gideon it was time to get in tune and in touch with who he was designed to be, a mighty man.

Gideon responded like so many of us do, with limiting stories of how we aren't much, but God said, "I will be with you."[8] Not only did he say that to Gideon, but he says that to us today.

It's time to exit the limiting stories that have blinded us from who we are and what we are to be. Gideon emerged from that cave with a newfound power, with an energy to lead his nation to a comeback and a turnaround, inspired and empowered by God.

It's interesting that God started a nation's comeback by changing the identity of one man. He knows if he can get you to see yourself through his eyes, you will be empowered to see God's greatness in the lives of others. The man and woman who perceive themselves as valuable will be willing to help others in practical ways, giving hope and help.

Action thought:

If I don't believe in myself, I don't properly believe in God. God can only do through me what I believe he will do.

Self-doubt

Don't let self-doubt debilitate, bury, and plague your potential. Understand how self-doubt personally affects you by thinking of it in these terms:

Self-doubt will torment me and prevent me. It prevents me by raising the obstacle of dread in my mind, where I think things won't work out so I don't want to try again. Self-doubt causes me to be double-minded and enslaved. It keeps me shackled in a prison of regret, chained to my then when I am living in my now. It keeps me shackled to who I used to be and the former label on me. Self-doubt tells me I have to determine my future by my past. It traps me and locks me into less; it causes me to play it safe, leaning on the familiar rather than taking a risk.

Refuse to be an inmate of your then when you're living in your now. It isn't God's plan for you to lack confidence. Confidence is something you can decide to have.

Aren't you glad God gives us a chance to escape the prison of regret and tap into tomorrow?

Enjoying yourself and others

Learn to be good with who God made you to be. Enjoy yourself.

If you don't enjoy yourself, you will end up rejecting yourself, dishonoring yourself, and presenting a pretend you.

It's time to agree with God and start feeling good about who you are. Certainly, you have some challenges and areas that could use improvement, but don't let those keep you from seeing yourself as righteous, forgiven, and capable.

It's important that you learn to feel good about yourself. Don't constantly listen to the accusing voice of your adversary, the devil, as he seeks to unravel your confidence and strength through his condemning conversations. Over and over, he will remind you of your shortcomings: the moment when you let anger get the best of you, you failed to help somebody, or you didn't follow through on your commitment to God. As a result, it's easy to live with a complex of guilt and condemnation that never allows you to enjoy your life.

Instead, embrace God's forgiveness and mercy. In truth, God is constantly shaping you and molding you into the person he wants you to be.

You're a work in progress. Let this knowledge give you a welcomed break from obsessing over all of your faults and flaws.

If we don't love ourselves, Jesus said we can't love others. If we don't have a healthy view and value for who we are, and if we don't learn to accept ourselves—faults, flaws, and all—we will never be able to properly love anyone else.

You must understand that you cannot give away what you don't have. If you don't love, appreciate, and respect yourself, you won't be able to love, appreciate, and respect others. In fact, you'll find yourself competing with them and complaining about them.

If you're experiencing a civil war on the inside, feeling angry and insecure about yourself, feeling unlovable and unattractive, then that is all you will give away.

On the other side of the coin, if you learn to love and accept what God loves and accepts in spite of your weaknesses, then you can give that love and value to the relationships in your life. This will change all of your relationships for the better.

If you see yourself as an unworthy recipient, you will reject the love, kindness, and goodness that people try to offer.

Everybody else is really not the problem; it's about you coming to peace with yourself. If you're negative toward yourself, negativity will flow into all of your relationships, including the one you have with God. You will never be able to fully enjoy what you have until you begin to enjoy who you are.

If you're a Christ-follower, you know God is in you and he is for you. If you begin to get that into your mentality and you begin to enjoy God and enjoy yourself, you'll begin to enjoy other people and appreciate them.

What is life without relationships? What, are you going to look at your trophies over and over and over again? I mean, that is cool for a minute, but really there isn't a whole lot of warmth found in looking at a fancy watch or at pictures of a trip if you have no one to enjoy them with.

We can only love other people as much as we love ourselves. We should love ourselves in a great and balanced way so we can love others in a great way.

Action thoughts:

What kind of relationship do I have with myself—am I more sin-conscious than righteousness-conscious?

Am I at peace with myself or do I always have to have the TV or radio on?

Why should I carry a constant sense of failure when all of us are in the process of becoming?

My capability and my potential are constant, but how much of it I use in my life will be dependent on how I view myself.

Baby elephants in the circus are trained at birth to be confined to a very small, limited place. Trainers use a rope to tie a baby elephant's leg to a strong wooden post placed firmly in the ground. This way, the baby elephant is confined to an area determined by the length of the rope. Though he attempts to break free from the rope, he soon learns it is too strong for his underdeveloped body, and over time, he allows its limiting length to define his comfort zone and his beliefs. Although that same elephant will grow to weigh up to five tons—strong enough to easily break the rope and find freedom beyond its limits—he won't even try to break it then because he has learned to believe he isn't able. Even the largest elephant can be confined and contained by a puny rope. Amazing![9]

Are you trapped by beliefs that keep your life within limits, when you have the potential for so much more?

Does this describe you? Are you trapped by beliefs that keep your life within limits, when you have the potential for so much more?

If I were to take your self-concept and put it into Michael Jordan's body, would he be able to hit the shot? If you had Kristi

Yamaguchi's physical skills but your mentality, would it work for you on an ice-skating rink? If you had to sing onstage during a business meeting to cinch a billion-dollar deal, would your mentality sabotage your ability? Embrace a deeper connection with who you are because your identity has a future. The question is, what will that future look like?

As you develop new beliefs of who you are from God's eye view, your behavior will change to support your new identity.

Action thought:

About a thousand days from now, I'm going to arrive three years into my future. What future is my current self-image building for me?

Self found

You have a treasure buried inside you. Let go of the labels and failures that limit you and that play with your destiny. Embrace an image of God that trumps every negative and allows you to live out of the positive; one that helps you rise after you fall.

If you're willing to change your thinking about yourself, God will change your life. Through a shift in your identity, you'll reconnect with a personal sense of destiny.

Destiny happens through decisions.

6

Power Moves

Everything in life is a choice. Our decisions, not conditions, shape our lives. No matter where we are or what we've been through, we have the power of choice to set a new outcome in motion.

All change begins with a personal choice to be committed to a certain result or a definite outcome. Therefore, it's important to know what you really value and what you really want. That way, you will know what to commit to.

Outcome living

Outcome living is being committed to a result, not to wishful thinking.

You have three options:

You can fortunetell—wish for change

You can foretell—see change in the future

You can forthtell—cause change through choice

Life doesn't get better by chance; life gets better by choice.

Decision brings the future into focus.

Decision removes confusion and gives clarity about what to do and how to do it. It clarifies what to embrace and what to let go of that no longer serves the real you. Clarity conserves energy for what really matters and eliminates minor things that will damage your life and wear you out if not dealt with and removed.

There is no escaping the truth that our decisions design and define our lives.

Call to action

Something you put off today will cost you an outcome tomorrow. If you were to put down this book right this second, what action would you take?

Would you go for a thirty-minute walk?

Would you pick up the phone and say "I love you" to somebody you haven't told that to in a long time?

Would you contact someone and forgive them?

Passive versus active choice

I don't want you to sit back as a passive observer for the rest of your life. Many people eventually succumb to a life that is full of passive choices, and they wonder why their lives have become so lazy and dull. It's because their lives are full of conditioned responses and apathetic attitudes.

We hear so many people talking about how tired and worn out they are, and I see this as a result of being reactive and passive, not active or penetrative. I want you to make active choices.

Passive choice = unmoved, lazy, neutral, dull, unassertive.

Neutral = a position that destroys effectiveness; excuses keep a person neutral.

Active choice = determined, on the offensive, assertive, forceful.

Results = the outcome or effect of a specific action, operation, plan.

Whatever you dream of becoming, today's decisions are tomorrow's reality. Every day that you excuse yourself from making a decision is a day you let the potential of another opportunity slip away from your life.

When you make a determined choice, not a passive one, you will live life looking to take radical action. When you're determined to lose weight, you will take your body to the gym and you will get in shape. When you're determined to live a good, enjoyable life, you will determine to be thankful and might even start writing down five things every morning that you're grateful for. A determined choice will cause you to take action.

Should never happens

I want you to live life by design where you are in the driver's seat. A lot of times, we say things such as, "Well, I should lose weight, I should call somebody, I should pray again, I should believe good things will happen to me, I should get up and comb my hair, I should clean all the junk out of garage."

We live every day saying "I should" do a million things, but should is not going to do anything other than cause you to should all over yourself. It will cause you to should on your dreams, should on your marriage, and ultimately, should all over your life.

"Well, I should take my wife out. I should go out of my way and wash her car. I should go to the dentist. I should read the Bible to bring faith into my heart. I should be positive. I should decide to get up and fight this depression. I should believe that this sickness will not end in death. I should…"

We have so many shoulds that our lives are shrouded in indecision.

Indecision paralyzes and inconveniences you. Indecision makes you a person that is reactive rather than active. It causes you to stay under stress and pressure. Indecision puts you on the defensive, instead of being on the offensive, assertive, and boldly moving toward something. Indecision causes drifting, and you can't drift forward in life, only backward.

If you're not driving forward and not making decisions about what you're going to go after (a committed outcome), you're just going to be driving around.

Excuses, excuses, excuses

When we have so many shoulds, we begin to live a life full of pity, marked by excuses about why we are and where we are.

On a personal level, this is what excuses look like:

Excuses keep me feeling powerless and stuck in neutral, in the place of indecision where life does something with me instead of me doing something with it.

Excuses don't excuse me, but accuse me and abuse me, and if I'm not careful, they will cause me to lose me.

Excuses cause me to become conditioned to a response where I am a victim, not a victor: I'm an addict because my daddy was an addict, I'm not smart because my mama wasn't smart, I'm not this because my family wasn't this.

Excuses are BS—belief systems that require no change.

They give me permission to stay where I am; a product of the past and a victim of the present.

Excuses give me permission to plateau where I am.

Excuses keep me pitiful rather than powerful.

They keep me bowing to the god of my feelings. Pity and excuses keep me out of the place I want to be. Together, they equal frustration.

Everyone has a pitiful story—a story that destroys them, dethrones them, and depletes them—but pitiful people major in what they don't have and what others haven't done for them. Pitiful people explore their pain and problems.

Excuses are decisions to suffer.

Disappointment, which everyone faces from time to time, can lead me into depression and despondency, abandoning me to a world of indecision about stepping out and attempting anything promising again. But the only power disappointment has in my life is the power I give to it. I can refuse to stay in a place of disappointment by deciding to live and act in God's reappointment.

Excuses keep me my vision hazy and my powers lazy.

Excuses keep me a can't person.

I don't have to be a can't person.

Can't people are resistant to opportunities, rationalize responsibility, refuse the personal cost to get involved, and replay problems. Do I find myself frustrated, murmuring, and complaining? I can choose to change the direction and the outcome of my life. I don't have to be a can't person.

Excuses give me "property poverty."

My property is my potential, gift, vision, and skills.

Excuses keep me stuck in deliberation.

Choosing causes me to collide with obstacles or opportunities, problems or possibilities. I can overcome the fear of making the wrong choice by making a choice. I can choose or lose.

While excuses wash us up by aging us, tiring us out, and breaking our will, making active choices wakes us up to act responsibly with our lives.

When God opens windows of opportunity for your growth and advancement, don't pull down the shades with excuses. Don't miss God by playing it safe. You can play it safe, and end up a year from now telling God you're sorry.

I Will

"I will" determines the quality and quantity of your life's experiences. "I would like" merely states an interest or a preference versus a commitment.

Life means risk. Without risk, you only have a near-life experience. Will you be a creature of circumstance or a creator of circumstances? Powerful people are those who have made up their mind to act.

Most people don't take action because they live worried about problems rather than committed to progress. Living out of feelings makes us focus on something without taking action and wastes all the ability inside of us.

Your potential takes shape after you make definitive choices to move in a certain direction. For example, when you commit to breaking the bondage of fear in your life, you will fight against fear.

To set yourself on the new track of achievement, accomplishment, and enjoyment your spirit craves, you're going to have to change the choices you've been making.

Choices have the ability to limit or lift our lives. Every person who accomplished something started right where they were with a decision.

Colonel Sanders started right where he was at sixty-five years of age when he decided to invest seventy-five dollars in a chicken recipe. Little did he know, that decision was going to have to go through 1,009 no's to get to his first yes from somebody who believed in his chicken recipe.[1] It's a good thing he didn't quit at 633. He kept going until he got a yes; he made a committed decision to turn his dream into reality.

Are you as committed as he was, or are you on a starvation diet where you've stopped feeding your dream and now you're feeding your doubt? You might say, "Well, maybe I'll try it another time." That's how we flirt with our dreams.

What kind of results are you committed to? Are you committed to having a high relationship with men and women in your life? Are you committed to having health? Are you committed to knowing God?

If you're not committed to results, tomorrow will come and you'll say, "I would like to have that..." All you're stating is something you think would be great in your life, a wish that will never become a reality. Reality is formed when decision is based on a commitment. "I commit to this result..." You become powerful in what you have committed to, not in what you are interested in.

When you commit, things will change! You'll get off drugs when you go to the right place, go through the treatment, and receive the power of God that sets you free. You'll become powerful in the gift the Lord has given you when you commit to your gift rather than date it. When you're committed to a great relationship with someone, you will look for ways to improve it and cause it to succeed.

Action thought:
Where will today's choices take me a year from now?

Learning to decide

How does someone learn to be decisive? By making decisions. There is no other way.

Until you start, you can't. You can't gain any muscle until you lift a weight. You can't walk until you take a step. There is no other way.

Let's start working those decision-making muscles; if you don't start somewhere, you're never going to build them. Why don't you start by making a decision right where you are?

Maybe a small decision. What is small decision you can make today to get moving in the right direction?

As you habitually exercise your decision-making muscles, they will develop in strength. As they grow stronger, you'll grow stronger.

When I started lifting weights, I couldn't lift the weight I can now. I can bench-press multiplied numbers more than I started with because I became good through repetition.

Action thoughts:

The reality of my life will change when I dare to make a decision. Decision is the very fabric that turns the invisible into reality.

Better choices, better outcomes

A principle from the book of Proverbs is to know the state of your life and attend to it. When someone doesn't attend to their life, it becomes overgrown with thorns, and thorns prick!

Have the thorns of life pricked you enough? Are you still tolerating things in your life that aren't comfortable and enjoyable? "Never complain about what you permit," says author Dr. Mike Murdock.

You must despise where you are to access where you want to go.

Through their leader, Joshua, God told the Israelite people, "Choose for yourselves this day whom you will serve."[2] You, too, can live your life doing what you feel like doing or you can live through God's inspiration breathing through you. Your life is way too wonderful to let an opinion other than God's decide how you will spend your days.

I want you to live life through wisdom. Wisdom looks beyond a situation to an outcome, a solution, a place of arrival. What is your life going to be devoted to? What will you value? *Is it something God would value in your life?*

If you pursue outcome, income will chase you down.

Unlock your outcome: Make a decision to think right thoughts, to forgive and forget, to give not just get.

Most people in our society are driven by income: "I want this, this person owes me." I don't want you to focus on income in your life because you need to focus on outcome. If you pursue outcome, income will chase you down.

Call to action

From this pivotal point in your life, what will you allow to drive you? (Guilt, fear, addiction to people's approval? Or faith, family, dreams?)

Inner power

What I'm excited about in your life right now is using your inner power to change your outer world.

Inner power is the place of making a new choice.

This is about owning your own life. This is where you fill in the blanks about how you will maximize the rest of your life so you don't have a near-life experience.

This is where you stop living by the way you feel. In fact, you're not what you feel; you're what you decide. You can feel elated and then feel exhausted within a minute. You can feel angry and then horny in a matter of seconds. Are you going to let how you feel run your life?

Why are so many New Year's commitments shot by February? Why do so many people enter rehab only to exit early? Why do so many people start marriage counseling, only to quit after the second week? Because people don't really make a commitment. Instead, they say, "I am going to try."

Trying something sets you up for failure because all you're stating is, "I would like this to happen and if it inconveniences me just a little, I'm not into it."

From Sigmund Freud's point of view, our lives are governed by the desire to gain pleasure and the desire to avoid pain.

We want to choose things that will give us pleasure. But not all of life is easy, so we can't make our choices based on pain avoidance.

No, empowered by God, you can work through the pain. If you choose to go with him, he will empower you to advance and triumph in the places of your personal adversity and challenge. I know you don't want any discomfort—we tend to want a big result without having to make any choices, hoping that God will do it if he wants it done.

No, you decide your outcomes; you determine the results you will receive.

Your habits will determine the quality of your life, so embrace some stop signs along the way. Stop overspending and overeating. Stop backbiting and complaining and talking about what was, and start talking about what can be.

You were created to be an initiator and an innovator. Until you change, nothing will change. As Gandhi said, "Be the change you want to see in the world." That takes some authenticity and assertive choice. Your feelings would love to talk you out of this, telling you that you don't need to do all that. Let me tell you, life isn't going to get better by doing nothing. A biblical principle says that when you work, you can have abundance, but if you don't work, you're chasing fantasies.[3]

You have no gain without some type of pain. "I don't want to sacrifice eating at McDonalds"— well, you're probably not going to have a healthy, long life. "I don't want to sacrifice my time to go to the gym four days a week" —well, you'll probably have problems with high blood pressure and heart failure.

When you're making decisions about your outcomes, ask yourself, what are the benefits to be gained and losses to be avoided? Looking at benefits to be gained and losses to be avoided will bring you to a place of inner power to change.

Nothing will change till you change, so you have to commit to actions and commit now. Procrastination makes difficulties grow! Procrastination cuts off your strength, your flavor, and your favor. Procrastination shortcuts you, and people who take shortcuts get cut short.

Call to action

What determined choices will you make at this moment? To imagine what you want, I've added some tips below to spur your imagination.

Income: What do you want? Why do you want it? What will it feel like to have it? When will you take action?

Tip: *If I read more, what will I gain?* (I will gain more knowledge, increase my skills, and make myself more valuable at work. I will enrich my income potential because I'm smarter and wiser at life's frequent crossroads.)

Career: What do you want? Why do you want it? What will it feel like to have it? When will you take action?

Tip: *If I don't believe the best about myself, how will this affect my performance? If I don't forgive someone at work, what will it cost me?*

Family and Friendships: What do you want? Why do you want it? What will it feel like to have it? When will you take action?

Tip: *If I don't believe the best about my spouse, what will my attitude cost my marriage? If I don't give up a habit of addiction, what will it cost my children?*

Health and Appearance: What do you want? Why do you want it? What will it feel like to have it? When will you take action?

Tip: *If I don't change my eating habits, what will it cost me? If I exercise, what will I gain?* (I will gain strength, a more alert mind, and a healthy body.)

Spiritual: What do you want? Why do you want it? What will it feel like to have it? When will you take action?

Tip: *If I don't pray, what will it cost me? What will I gain if I read the Bible?*

Your decisions will determine your destiny and your destination. Stand up on the inside; realize and release your inner powers to change your outer world.

7

Breaking Through

Success is intentional. It is the result of deliberate decision.

Your ability to succeed is inside you; it's a seed given by God. For it to grow, you must plow, plant, and water. After that, you get to reap a harvest.

Plowing is breaking ground. In your life, plowing is raising the standard, where you say there is more to life and this is what it looks like.

To raise your level of excellence, you're going to have to let go of some things that are hindering your ability to take forward action. Let me ask, what are three things you have to eliminate right away? (This might be relationships, eating habits, spending habits, or viewing habits).

Planting is where you make a decision to invest in your gift.

For me, this began many years ago when I walked away from a professional baseball contract after having a spiritual encounter with God. As I've already mentioned, it happened to me on an airplane as I sat beside a seventy-six-year-old Texas woman named Louise Hicks. I was on my way to my second year of spring training with the Boston Red Sox in Fort Myers, Florida.

I put a big dip of Copenhagen in my lip and I opened the green Bible my grandpa gave me when I was nine years old. As I began to read, the lady next to me said, "Are you into that thing?" I said, "I'm trying to be." For the next few hours, she gave me help and wisdom and insight. She said, "The God of that Bible is going to transform your life." Without knowing me, she began to prophecy about everything concerning the big future that awaited me.

Interestingly, she stayed after me even after I got to spring training. Every couple of days I would receive a letter from her saying, "You can't give up, you're more than a conqueror through Christ." She started reinforcing who I was in God, and reading her letters would always cause so many tears in my eyes that I would have to take the letters into a bathroom stall where no one could see me. I would listen to "Knockin' On Heavens Door" by Guns N' Roses, (and yes, I still like Guns N' Roses), and I would lift my hands and start singing it. I would read Louise's handwritten letters and I would begin to cry and weep.

She would write, "People are waiting for you. People need you. Your life is going to touch a lot of people. You are going to change people with the power of God. There are so many people you are going to impact and transform." I imagined doing that at night instead of going out to the clubs.

After being released by the Boston Red Sox, I went and played in Canada for a season. I was drafted in the first round of an independent professional league, but my desire to help people began to outweigh my desire to play baseball.

I decided I would ask my grandpa if maybe I should go to a Bible school. He said, "Why don't you try it and see if you're into it?" I went in and I flunked. I wasn't cut out for it. Still, I was having these really wonderful experiences with God and trying to decide, where do I go from here? where do I go to touch and help people?

I decided to work as a janitor in my grandpa's church, and I began to feel in my heart that I needed to walk away from baseball. People who knew me probably thought, man, he's lost his mind. They asked me, "Why in the world would you walk away from something you've devoted your life to?" I had given my life to baseball hour after hour after hour. I was the kid who was up at six thirty or seven o'clock in the morning, taking three hundred ground balls before school started, then working at it again late at night, five nights a week.

Sometimes you got to think big in small places.

But the voice of the lady I met on the plane kept echoing, "You will touch people." Working as a custodian didn't offer such a promising future—as my friend Tim Storey says, "Sometimes you got to think big in small places." That's where you are, and that's okay because the Bible says never despise a day of small beginnings.[1] Everything big started as something small. Small beginnings shape you and make you for big futures. God never puts in the light what he doesn't shape in the dark, and what he sees in the dark he always rewards in the light.

As I was scrubbing toilets that smelled really bad and picking up gum off the floors, I decided to work in the kids' department. I taught the kids about Jonah and the whale. I probably missed it a couple times when I told them about Shamu the whale and Flipper the dolphin, but I had fun throwing them some toy fishies and trying to tell Bible stories. I was investing in their lives.

Without planting, there is no harvest. A seed is powerless until it is planted. Inside of the seed is a tree, and inside of the tree is a whole forest. Within the forest are books, newspapers, and magazines. This book was once a seed.

Your life is powerless until it is planted. Are you going to plant yourself anywhere? If you're always implanted in the realm of indecision, your life will never take shape. The soil of determination and decision releases action, feeling, and sensation—relationally, spiritually, and emotionally.

Since I had keys to the church, I would go there around eleven thirty at night and sing songs to God. I would sit there and imagine what the lady from the plane said I could do. One night I thought, man, I'm going to start practicing! That's when I started planting seed. In my grandfather's church, there were two thousand seats. I got up behind the podium and pretended to speak to thousands of people. I motivated the carpet, I inspired the empty seats, I made the chandeliers cry.

I did something most people never do—I prepared. It's as if we want the stage of life but don't want the dress rehearsal. If you never prepare your lines and learn from your rehearsal, when the stage comes, you won't even be ready for the dressing room.

I remember those days of working at it, planting my seed. *I gave myself to my gift.*

When you make a decision to start somewhere, you might not get the most desirable start. You might have to work at a job you don't like as you work your dream at home. Why don't you let your job pay for your dream? Go do your job well, putting value and honor into it and succeeding with people. Increase always comes through the people in your life.

Give yourself time, and commit every day to working on your dream. Maybe your dream is to build your own auto shop and run it one day. Maybe it's to teach learning disabled kids. Maybe it's to design the next technological breakthrough. Whatever it is, I've noticed that we become good at what we give ourselves to, which confirms something interesting: everybody arrived here on earth with something on the inside of them to help others.

Your skills and talents benefit others and bring increase to you. All of your potential and passion are built around your God-given gift, skills, and abilities. If you never give yourself to them, you'll never walk out of where you are right now, you'll never create room for higher relationships, and you'll never see the best new opportunities.

Watering means staying at it, like a farmer who believes for a harvest. He keeps watering the seed, especially during the dry seasons, even though he hasn't yet seen a plant emerge from the seed he planted.

I heard a story about Michael Jackson. By the age of ten, he would take a little board with him on Sundays when his family would go to Quincy Jones's house for lunch. The kids would go out and play on the jungle gym, but Mike used to take his little board off to the side and work on a dance. All the other kids would say, "Michael, come join us," but he would say, "No, I'm working on something."

Michael would be off to the side, moving his legs in a backward motion, trying to develop a dance. He worked on this dance at age ten, eleven, twelve, thirteen, fourteen, fifteen, sixteen, seventeen, eighteen, nineteen, twenty, twenty-one, twenty-two, twenty-three and twenty-four. At twenty-four, the young man kids joked with about that board he kept working with came out with a dance called the Moonwalk and a sparkly sock and a diamond glove. Now millions applaud it and try their best to imitate it. Michael stayed at it, never giving up.

It's one thing to start something; it's another to stay at it.

You won't be known by what you start, only by what you finish. Don't settle for false finish lines in your life; stay at it until you've succeeded.

Your enemy, the devil, is always out to wear you out, tire you out, and exhaust you. He wants you to think you've been through too much, you've come too far; you can quit and just play it easy now.

But you've come too far to quit now! You have to get that eye of the tiger and say, "This is the last round! I'm going to give it one more shot. I'm going to jump back into the ring and I'm going to take a swing because it's my time to begin to dance and sing. This is my moment!"

You plow, you plant, you water, and then you reap. Reaping is obtaining.

Think about it. In your life right now, you are reaping some good things you've sown. Enjoy and be grateful; don't be all work and no play.

We can get so focused on preparing for event after event that we never enjoy now. I don't want you to do that. I want you to prepare for more and work for the future you want, but enjoy the present. Be at peace with yourself. Enjoy some of the blessings of your current harvest, while envisioning your future harvest.

As a child, my brother Russell and I were really into the World Wrestling Federation. One year, we convinced our dad to buy WrestleMania so we could watch Hulk Hogan wrestle Andre the Giant in a pay-per-view match.

Our father told us it was a fixed fight; it was already determined who would win. He told us that at a certain time in the match, there would be a shift of momentum and Hulk Hogan would unexpectedly come out on top.

So we intently watched that TV screen, as Hulk Hogan got beat up by Andre the Giant. As blood squirted everywhere, we thought, how much more can this man take?

All of a sudden, Hulk Hogan caught his breath and started shaking his arms, while standing there in his yellow briefs. The crowd started rallying as he continued to shake. We thought, this is miraculous—this is the greatest comeback ever!

Our parents started laughing because they knew this comeback was part of a predetermined plan.

Hulk Hogan won, and my brother and I screamed!

Life is the same way. When you plow, plant, and water, God has determined a certain season for things to shift and for you to reap.

You've already made the determined decision to plow, thereby raising the standard in your life. Now as you plant (work on your gift) and water (stay at it), things will start turning in your favor. As they do, it's important for you to understand true success.

8

Wealth

Your valuables do not determine your value. Your riches do not determine your wealth.

Riches are what you have, but wealth is who you are.

How does a person become wealthy? By developing an excellent spirit.

"Excellence" means "valuable quality: virtue."[1] Excellence is not a skill, but an attitude from the heart. Excellence means you ask more of yourself than others do. Excellent people value others.

You're an excellent person if you care more than others think is wise, if you risk more than others think is safe, if you do more than others think is practical, and if you expect from God more than is naturally possible.

Excellence distinguishes a person. In the job market, excellence allows a person with an attitude of service to get a job over someone more qualified. That's because employers know that excellent employees don't just sell a product; they give customers an experience.

We all give an experience. Let me ask you, what is the experience you're consistently giving to people you're in contact with?

I met a young contractor who was trying to expand his business around an average idea. While listening to me speak, he repositioned his viewpoint. He took the message about giving people an experience of wealth and decided to see how he could improve the businesses of the people he wanted to contract with. He called each of them and asked, "How can I help your business?" Then he gave them the knowledge and opportunity to improve their businesses.

As a result, the first week he landed a contract of $89,000. The second week, he landed a $171,000 contract. The fourth week, he landed a $223,000 contract. He went from being unable to pay his bills to making $483,000 in one month because he changed his approach. He stopped passively soliciting contracts and started actively giving a positive experience.

What's the difference between the doctor and the gardener? They're both of equal value as people, but since the doctor gives a more valuable experience and contribution to the people around him, he makes more money. The key to your increase is to enhance the experience you give to the world around you.

I saw Oprah Winfrey interviewing Sean "Diddy" Combs, the hip-hop mogul, who is now worth hundreds of millions of dollars. Growing up in a poor neighborhood, with limited means, limited education, and limited surroundings, he had to "go within" or go without. At his job, he gave himself to being the best at customer service. People always wanted him around because of the experience he gave them. He would always outdo their requests, so he became an asset in their eyes.

When we have an excellent spirit, we prepare to bring more knowledge than is required to help people, and that preparation distinguishes us. Didn't God call us to be a light? To stand out, not just blend in? By doing so, we're bringing something that is a cut above the rest.

Enhance the experience you give to the world around you.

If we're not investing in people, we're using them. We're just consumers, merely swallowing them up.

Action thought:

Do I punch in at the clock and consume my employer's time just to get a paycheck, or am I there to invest?

Winning with people

When people notice your excellent attitude, you'll begin to win with people, and the more you win with people, the more opportunities and advancements will open up to you.

Winning with people determines increase in every area of your life. You win with people by the words you speak and by the way you present yourself. Even though you may want to dress the way you feel most comfortable, let me tell you, there are places and faces that will bring increase in your life that you can't get to if you don't conform to their standard of appearance. Sometimes it's good to honor other people's standards.

Have you noticed most people don't smile? Practice smiling—people will genuinely want to be close to you. By smiling, you'll give people an experience where they feel at ease and encouraged.

Look for what's right in somebody. My wife and I go to restaurants and often say to each other, "Let's find something great about our waiter or waitress." When we notice something, we tell them how much we appreciate it.

All through the day, whether I'm in a hotel lobby or whether I'm on an airplane, I always try to find something great about someone. Sometimes that means putting a little pat on their back and saying, "Hey, it's good to see you today" or "Man, thank you so much for going the extra mile."

People get discouraged; therefore, we can cause a better future for them by being voices that create hope and expectation. I want to stir you to notice and be grateful for what others bring to your life. When someone does anything nice for you, let that person know you appreciate it. If you ate at a restaurant recently, did you thank the waiter for filling your coffee cup the second time without being asked? If you took the bus today, was it on time? If so, did you thank the driver?

Let me let you in on an effective key to revolutionize your life: There is real power in being thankful and appreciative. When you express appreciation, not only does it empower the people who hear your words, but it also releases joy inside of you. You'll find that whatever you will praise, you will raise.

Are you a thankful person, or are you going so fast you can't see the blessing around you until it's too late? Look around at your loved ones and coworkers and be thankful. Slow down and see the blessing.

Action thoughts:

Do I give people more pressure and worry, or do I alleviate it?
Do I listen quickly and speak slowly with my friends, family, and colleagues?

You and I have a responsibility to give people an experience that values and improves them. Jesus did this through asking questions. As a child, do you remember people often asking, "Who do you want to be?" But after growing up, the question changed to merely, "How are you doing?"

By presenting better questions to people in your personal and professional relationships, you will immediately engage them and bring an abundance of opportunity to all of your lives. This is because questions convey respect (I value your opinion and I'm waiting for an answer), questions convey connection (ensuring two-sided conversations), and questions transmit continuation (they open up a dialog where ideas have a chance to grow, breathe, and mature).

If you generate questions around three main areas—finances, family, and fitness—people will express their dreams and then you will know how to best serve them. That way, your relationship will grow.

We can also ask ourselves better questions such as, how can I improve a friend's life, how can I improve my marriage, and how can I improve my business—always looking for something to give rather than take.

Accustomed to a lifestyle of text messages and e-mails, it's easy to forfeit personal interaction. What if we improved our excellence by going the extra mile? What if we picked up the phone to ask, "How is your day going?"

Set yourself in motion today to create increase in the lives around you. As you do, people will begin to rise up to help you, creating more opportunities for your life.

Increase and advancement in our lives is always related to the people in our lives. If we avoid people, we avoid increase.

Leaving a memorable impression

Crowds of people thronged Jesus because he kept giving them an experience they wanted. In one instance, he was at a wedding where he turned water into wine. Another time, he restored sight to a man who had known physical blindness his whole life. To a woman who was about to be stoned for committing adultery, he quickly intervened by opposing her accusers and offering her forgiveness and a new lease on life. All of his power would have remained dormant if he hadn't chosen to value people and give them the experience they needed.

The value we put on someone leaves a memory they'll want to revisit.

Ask yourself, am I giving people an experience where they feel my genuine concern and excellence, or am I giving them an experience they would rather not endure again?

In my travels, I've endured flights where someone on board smells badly and the experiences have always left me thinking that it will be tough for anyone to want to get to know those individuals. They gave experiences I didn't want to have again.

Ty Cobb was definitely one of the greatest baseball players who ever lived and played the game. As a former professional baseball player myself, I am very aware of his accomplishments. He set over ninety records in his amazing career, yet his interpersonal relationships suffered. Only three baseball players attended his funeral.

How sad that a man could achieve so much, yet be loved and valued by so few in his profession. Whether or not he fit the description of a fool isn't my call to make, but certainly, foolish relational choices left bad memorable impressions.

When we act wisely, we gain favor with those around us. At work, wise decisions bring value to the table, resulting in awards, bonuses, and pay increases. The book of Proverbs says, "The wise inherit honor."[2]

When we act wisely, we gain favor with those around us.

Wise choices leave a good memorable impression.

Action thoughts:

What kind of taste do I leave in people's mouths? Is it one they want to savor or is it one they want to spit out?

Get rich quick

Wise people set their focus on giving rather than getting.

This is unpopular and contrary to what most books say today, but the book that has sold the most copies and was inspired and endorsed by God says not to wear ourselves out trying to get rich, but to use some wisdom and show some restraint instead.

"Cast but a glance at riches, and they are gone, for they will surely sprout wings and fly off to the sky like an eagle" (Prov.

23:5 NIV). If you think about the times you've invested in things with the intent of getting rich, you'll remember that most of the time you lost your investments. On the other hand, when you kept your focus on achieving an outcome through labor, you usually had more success than you had imagined.

Everyone wants to win the lottery. Everyone wants to get rich with as little effort as possible, but out of 50 million people who hold a lottery ticket, 49,999,999 people will throw their tickets in the trash. The same is true about the get-rich-quick schemes; for every single winner, there are millions of losers.

On the other hand, one hundred out of one hundred people who apply diligence to give people an excellent experience through their labor will ultimately succeed. Although it involves more effort, the odds of the high life are a whole lot better.

"Wealth from get-rich-quick schemes quickly disappears" (Prov. 13:11 NLT).

What we don't value, we violate

If we chase income instead of outcome, we violate our integrity, our character, the trust people have in us, our bodies, and our common sense. A person who hastens to be rich won't be found innocent.[3]

If we're looking to gain material possessions, we're not looking to give to people, and eventually, we'll feel unfulfilled.

Is this you?

Surely you wouldn't cheat yourself in life by just taking, taking, and taking some more, and never giving what people need, would you? If all you're doing is consuming, then you're so driven by income that outcome keeps eluding you. Proverbs 10:22 says the blessing of the Lord brings wealth and he doesn't add any sorrow with it, but you'll find that you have money with much sorrow; you have opportunities, but you don't enjoy them—all because you keep requiring more things. Face it, you're materialistic.

People who chase income experience a short-lived success, and that success includes much sorrow because income chasers cheat people. They take shortcuts that cut them short of the fulfillment they desire. Income chasers are actually influenced by a spirit of greed.

Remember this: Love gives, but lust takes.

Giving conquers greed

Do you ever find yourself contemplating a compromise, being tempted to chase income instead of outcome? Close your eyes to compromise, or greed will begin to take over your life.

When a seed of greed takes root, we begin to pursue our careers with such fervency that we begin to neglect the very people we wanted to provide for. "A greedy man brings trouble to his family" (Prov. 15:27 NIV). There is no such thing as "my own business" because what we do affects everyone we care about. It doesn't matter what we're greedy for—more money, more possessions, or more drugs or alcohol to serve an addiction. And greed can distort relationships with spouses and children through possessiveness, which shows up as wanting more time and attention than another person is able to give.

Driven by income, greedy people create more and more projects that cause them to sacrifice their families, health, vitality, enjoyment, creativity, and intuitiveness. They substitute quality of life for quantity of life.

Proverbs 1:19 NLT says, "Such is the fate of all who are greedy for money; it robs them of life." That sounds like an empty life; one that is lacking fulfillment, full of conflict, and full of turmoil.

Howard Hughes was driven by greed; he was driven by income—money, power, and fame—and not outcome. He was known as the richest man in the world, yet he had no lasting happiness, fulfillment, or security. He could have had anything and lived anywhere, yet he spent the last years of his life in extreme isolation, wildly afraid.

We may acquire whatever we're greedy for, but the Word of God promises that even when we acquire it, we will have nothing of value. Greed steals our happiness and reason for living because we can't be happy or fulfilled when our focus is on what we don't have. We lose our former purpose for living because now our lives center on chasing what we lack.

Greed steals our integrity. Greed is never patient. Greed wants instant gratification; it creates the attitude "I want as much as I can get, and I want it now." Greed never ends.

No matter what you get, do you soon want more? Do you compromise your ethics to get what you want? Are you experiencing less contentment and fulfillment?

If you find yourself experiencing more conflict in life, consider whether or not you're continually thinking about *what you don't have*. Thinking about lack can create turbulence in your life, and turbulence can be a signal that greed is overtaking you.

The good news is, once you become aware of this tendency toward greed, you can hit the breaks and slam it in reverse. You can have both quality and quantity of life if you fight greed as an enemy.

To remove greed once you've been infected by it, set your focus on giving generously to the needs of others. Proverbs 21:26 says the righteous person gives without sparing.

Greed is the illness; generosity is the cure.

The fastest way to eliminate greed from your life is to make a concentrated effort to give. You don't have to wait until you become rich to become generous. Become generous with your time, kindness, words, encourage- ment, love, labor, and possessions.

Call to action

Let this be the moment when you say, "I'm going to raise my level of excellence—I'm going to upgrade my giving."

You don't have to wait until you become rich to become generous.

Unlock and unleash wealth

There are no poor people on this planet; only unaware people who don't realize the wealth of God inside of them.

You have a gold mine inside of you.

Every one of us can improve the quality of life of people around us, even in little ways. God is pleased when we give. He is pleased when we prosper in all ways and when we become a channel of prosperity to others around us.

Why invest your life in things that depreciate rather than in giving that appreciates?

$\mathcal{9}$

Power Talk

Words are the most powerful tool in the whole world. They shape the course of our destiny.

A professional fighter came to me and said, "Would you come see my mom? She's in the hospital."

"What's wrong with her?"

"She has Lupus, and she slipped into a coma after surgery. She hasn't responded in over a week."

I said I would definitely come, and I traveled to the hospital with my assistant and her husband. When we got to the hospital, they took us to ICU. On the wall, we saw glowing pictures of the fighter's mother as a former Miss Universe. Now, looking at her in a hospital bed, I saw a woman who wasn't conscious, but incoherent and unresponsive to the people she loved.

With the doctors in the room, we all gathered around the hospital bed. I said, "Before we pray and ask God to heal her, why don't we lift our hands and thank God for being so nice to us?" We lifted our hands and thanked God for being a healer and a peacemaker. We thanked him for hearing our prayers and responding to us. We thanked him for being a God who is merciful and who makes a way where there is no way.

Suddenly, the woman reached up and pulled my arm down! She had completely come out of the coma.

Over the next couple of days, her strength returned. She got up out of bed and walked. She left the hospital and lived her life.

Telling God thank you has power!

To feed a crowd of over five thousand, Jesus only had five loaves of bread and two fish.[1] The first thing he did was shift his satellite receiver to the "All Things Are Possible Network" and thank his Father. The minimal amount of food miraculously stretched to feed the crowd, with twelve basketfuls left over. Instead of looking at the size of the problem, Jesus looked to the solution by first thanking God.

I wonder if God has miracles in motion for your life, but all they need to materialize is for you to give expression to them rather than to the problems and challenges you're currently facing.

Could there be a miracle God has already set in motion over your life? There was a miracle over Lazarus to get him out of the tomb, but he needed Jesus to call him out. Maybe now is the time for you to become solution-minded and speak the end result.

Could there be a miracle in motion over your children? Rather than talking about what they don't do right, talk great about them. Remember, potential rises to the level of communication placed upon someone.

What about your finances? Maybe you're working hard but the ends still don't meet and you don't see a way to solve it. Why don't you say, "God is able to create avenues of revenue for me. He will connect me to the right people in the right places." Then start looking for it to happen. It's amazing how God meets you when you're expectantly looking.

Action thoughts:

Instead of talking about my problems, what if I focused on thanking God for the solutions? What if I talked about how grateful I am that God is on my side?

Thanking God will relax and revitalize you and turn obstacles into opportunities. Thanking God releases miracles.

Words empower

Did you know your mind and mouth are connected? Words we speak program our thoughts and actions; therefore, those who say they *can* and *can't* are right.

Words spoken today determine experiences both today and in the future; they either put us into or take us out of position to receive good things from God.

Words possess creative ability; they're carriers of life and death.

Words are like seeds that produce fruit in our lives and the lives of others.

Words stir up emotion and cause action. Words are containers that inflame or injure, eliminate love or elevate it.

Words shape and change our beliefs.

Words take on a life of their own because they carry the power to liberate or limit. Words create positive or negative momentum.

Words build or destroy, heal or hurt, deliver or defeat, empower or impoverish.

Words lift marriages and dreams.

Words are like a thermostat: while a thermometer reveals the temperature of a room, a thermostat sets the atmosphere to a comfortable temperature. Negative words pollute the atmosphere of our lives and the lives of others, while words that thank God bring miracles.

Our words set in force a chain of events that affect our stress level, the direction we head, and the quality of our relationships.[2]

I've learned, I can't have a negative mouth and a positive life.

One of the most empowering insights of my life came when I stumbled upon a treasure in the Word of God recorded in Philemon 1:6 that says our faith becomes "effectual by the acknowledging of every good thing which is in [us] in Christ Jesus." Well then, the opposite is true: our fear becomes effective and powerful by acknowledging every bad or wrong thing in us. Therefore, we must begin to eliminate negative, pitiful talk and embrace power talk.

We must begin to eliminate negative, pitiful talk and embrace power talk.

Powerless talk

Have you been saying, "I think I'll never get out of debt"? Or "I know my marriage will end in divorce"? Or "I guess I'll have to put up with this health problem the rest of my life"? When you talk like this, you become your own worst enemy.

Many people live down and out as a result of saying words like these:

Nothing good ever happens to me.

I don't have what it takes.

I can't do it.

I'll never get out of this.

Powerless talk is full of defeat, failure, fear, talking about the enemy, and what is holding us back. When we talk of failure, we invite it to rule us and keep us trapped. When we speak words of fear, we increase our awareness of its paralyzing power as it sabotages the success we want.

Multitudes of people fail in life because they talk failure and defeat. They talk failure and defeat because that's what's inside their hearts—they believe in it.

According to Luke 6:45, if our talk is full of negative and confusing things, it's because our hearts are that way. If we talk fear, sickness, poverty, and anxiety, our words are painting a true picture of what we really believe about our lives.

Words of unbelief, negativity, sickness, and fear guarantee a miserable life.

As long as we talk weakness, poverty, sickness, and defeat, we will continue to experience them. A negative mouth can pollute our mind, attitude, atmosphere, and mood with heaviness, discouragement, and defeat.

One reason God gave us a tongue is so we could design and create a better world for ourselves, and we do this by speaking his words that are alive and full of faith, health, and power. The Bible says, "The words of the reckless pierce like swords, but the tongue of the wise brings healing," so if we're wise, we'll speak words of health, life, and healing.[3] That way, we'll speak God's promise in the face of apparent defeat.

How much of our anxiety stems from our conversations? We talk about how tired we are, injustices in our workplaces, the high stress level our kids cause us, and having too much to do. Since words are seeds that produce after their own kind, talking about pressure produces more anxiety than we had to begin with.

"Anxiety in the heart of man causes depression, but a good word makes it glad"; so according to God's view, good words remove anxiety and make the heart glad again.[4] Good refers to something agreeable, something pleasant, and something suitable. A positive person can design their world with words that produce love, joy, and positive expectation.

You might find yourself in some very difficult circumstances where things don't look too promising, and it would be very tempting just to complain and curse, but if you speak words of failure and defeat, you'll become more discouraged and less confident because your words will become self-fulfilling prophecies.

Lessons learned

When a coach, teacher, or parent doesn't understand the potential in children, but only looks at their current behavior, repeatedly telling them how they never measure up without honoring anything positive, their spirits will begin to break down and they'll begin to look for what is wrong with themselves rather than what is right.

Years ago, a study took a look at a group of children who were the poorest students and put them in a classroom with the top teachers. Those conducting the study told the teachers to challenge the students by telling them they were the most highly developed students in the school and that their role as teachers was to stretch them further. Through these positive words, they spoke to the students on a higher level. At the end of the study, these kids measured at the top of their class with all A's and B's. Beforehand, they had been getting D's and F's.[5]

Our level of communication has a large effect on our physical performance. Before his personal challenges, Tiger Woods didn't talk to himself about his challenges in hitting a golf ball, because from the age of four, his father spoke words that told him he was the greatest golfer in the world. Consequently, Tiger Woods kept telling himself, "I'm Tiger Woods, the greatest golfer in the world. I make these shots, I drill this putt." He didn't allow other people's voices to distract him. He spoke his own world into existence, and became the greatest golfer in the world. Since his personal troubles began, other people's voices seem to have become a distraction and his own comments about his game have changed. This resulted in 2010 being the worst season in his career.

Words stir potential and faith. God speaks to a person's potential so they move beyond where they are to experience something new. I wonder what would happen if we followed his example by speaking well of ourselves and others—would our relationships, self-confidence, and enjoyment improve both in quality and quantity?

Don't waste your breath

We must learn to master our mouths: we can speak what we currently have and see it grow or we can speak about what we want to see in our lives and watch our faith go to work to see those outcomes.

If you don't manage your mouth, your words will minimize your enjoyment.

If you don't manage your mouth, your words will minimize your enjoyment. Through managing your speech, you will replace frustration, discouragement, hopelessness, loneliness, sickness, anxiety, bad habits, and guilt with hope, vision, new friends, and good habits.

I wonder... Rather than agonizing in prayer for something to change, if you began speaking about what God can pull off in your life, would that bring the results you want?

We can almost pray our way out of faith by focusing on a problem so much that we actually depress and overwhelm ourselves. Jesus never prayed long prayers. If you really want to look at a person who mastered the tough elements of life such as lack and disease, look at Jesus, who always spoke the solution and end result, never the problem. Living that way allowed him to live with energy and momentum toward the end result instead of being stuck on a problem.

Jesus dominated disease and demons, all through the power of his mouth. His inspired words changed the course of life for everybody he encountered.

Shifting from negative words to positive words benefits you. Do you often say you're a failure, afraid, confused, not feeling well, or overwhelmed? Start saying, "I'm learning and failing forward, I am strong in God, and I don't live in a spirit of fear." Do you say "I hate..." a lot? Instead, say, "I prefer when this happens."

I want you to stop cursing yourself with "I can't do this." Instead of magnifying the problem, state the end result. People who perform at a top level talk about what they will do, not about what they can do. Convinced people talk about what will be; unconvinced people talk about what can be.

Positive minds and mouths experience positive lives. Positive mouths are full of faith and hope.

Eliminate: I can't, If, I don't think, I don't have the time, I'm afraid of, I don't believe, It's impossible

Add: I will, I know, I am confident, I do believe, God is able

Call to action

Do you compliment yourself or do you constantly confront yourself with communication that lessens you in your own eyes?

What five words do you say that make you make feel powerless? Powerful?

Maybe you're in a place of despair, facing a seemingly insurmountable problem. Well, God is with you and he is a miracle-working God with a reputation for doing things that defy logic!

Don't waste your words describing your situation; use your words as a tool to change your situation. Living will become a pleasure through power talk.

10

Words for the Wise

I heard a story about John Osteen, the father of Joel Osteen the famous "happy preacher," that went something like this. Years ago, the devil appeared in a vision and said, "I'm going to kill you. I'm going to destroy your family." As the devil kept taking steps toward him, John kept taking steps backward. All of a sudden, Jesus showed up in the vision and said, "Get him!" John said, "Jesus, you get him." Jesus stood next to John and started taking steps backward with him.

John did what many of us often do. We say, "Get my marriage, God. Get my boss—you know how grouchy he is! Get my banker, get my dentist, get my finances..." and we keep taking steps backward.

So Jesus kept taking steps backward with John, and John was perplexed because the more he said, "Jesus, get him, get him, destroy him," the more Jesus kept taking steps backward.

Then Jesus took one last step, but instead of taking a step backward, he took a step into John's body and said, "Now you get him, in my name!" As soon as John stepped forward and spoke in Jesus' name, the enemy vanished. Until John came into agreement with God and spoke against the devil, nothing changed.

The Bible says two people can't make progress until they're in agreement. Part of agreeing is saying the same thing as each other. We have the choice to agree with and say the same things as our challenging circumstances, or to agree with and speak the solutions from God's Word.

The question is, who will you agree with?

To experience a life lift, value God's Word on your lips. Speak in line with God's Word. Here are some compelling reasons:

1. "The speech of the upright rescues them" (Prov. 12:6 NIV).

2. "If you live in Me [abide vitally united to Me] and My words remain in you and continue to live in your hearts, ask whatever you will, and it shall be done for you" (John 15:7 AB).

3. "Do not let this Book of the Law depart from your mouth; meditate on it day and night, so that you may be careful to do everything written in it. Then you will be prosperous and successful" (Josh. 1:8 NIV).

God's Word reveals his thoughts and will (or intention).

Acknowledge the good things about yourself in Christ. *Train yourself to speak right. Speak God's language.*

When God made the world, he did it by speaking words. Since we're made in his image, we create with our words, too.

When we talk, we are always speaking our world into existence, so let's speak it as we wish it to be.

If you want your life to improve, do what God does: Call those good things that don't exist as if they did. You will change your life by changing your vocabulary to match God's.

Change your life by changing your vocabulary.

What are God's words? You'll find them in the Bible. For example, if you're discouraged, the Bible says, "Why, my soul, are you downcast? Put your hope in God."[1] From this scripture, you can say, "I hope in God."

If you're feeling hatred toward someone, the Bible says, "God's love has been poured out into our hearts," so you can say, "I love (and fill in the blank)."[2]

If Jesus were to step out of the pages of this book right now and say, "Everything you say from this moment forward will happen just the way you say, both good and bad," would that change the way you speak about your work, your health, your family, your finances? I think it would.

A miracle is on its way

Sitting at lunch one day with a friend of mine named Mike, a man who's a designer for rap artists and NBA stars, he said, "Will you come pray for my mom's friend?" She was dying of cancer at a cancer research hospital in Seattle, Washington.

I said, "Let's do it. We'll get another flight because this is important—she's at death's door."

So we got there and they sent us upstairs where they were doing the chemo treatments. Apparently, she always got her chemo treatment out in the hallway or in a bigger room with everybody, but this day she had her own room. I walked in and here was this woman, sitting there shivering with tubes inserted into her for treatment.

She said, "I am so glad to see you! Today is going to be a great day! I needed my own room today to give me my own space because a miracle is going to happen! I know God is going to do a miracle. I told the nurses a miracle worker is coming." The nurses were there in the room.

I said, "God wants to help you and something good is going to happen to you today. We need to make sure that any hurt or resentment you have in your heart toward anybody or anything is gone. I don't want that to clog you up from receiving the goodness of God into your life. Make sure you forgive people, and also receive Jesus' forgiveness because we have all sinned against God. I'm going to lead you in prayer to receive Jesus' life and presence."

Through words, I helped her receive God's life. Through words, she released all the hurt, pain, and inner turmoil in her heart, and all the bitterness and grudges she had held against people.

Next I told her I would begin praying for her healing. I said, "God, I thank you for your healing powers flowing through her. I thank you, God, for the solution. Thank you, Jesus, for removing every bit of cancer. She created space for you to heal her because she spoke a miracle into existence in her life today. I thank you that your healing powers are flowing through her blood and through her body and that she is being made whole, in Jesus' name."

She said she felt a warm sensation going into her body. Five days later, she walked out of that hospital with no trace of cancer, all because she spoke her expectation.

Are your words working for you or against you?

What do you want?

The Spice Girls sang a song called "Wannabe" years ago that said, "Tell me what you want, what you really really want."

What do you really, really want? One of the best ways to find out what you want is to say what you don't want. Afterward, saying what you do want creates positive momentum in your life.

"I don't want to be fat."

Why don't you want be fat? "Because I want to be healthy, I want to be strong, and I want to feel good."

"I don't want to be sick."

Why don't you want to be sick? "Because I want to enjoy my kids, I want to enjoy my grandkids, I want to be able to walk, I want to be able to talk, I want to be able to think, I want to be able to express myself."

"I don't want to be ignorant."

Why don't you want to be ignorant? "Because I want to be able to have a good job, I want to be able to grow, and I want to be able to expand."

He said, she said

What we dish out is what we're going to eat.

The words we speak have power to influence people's lives around us, either endangering or enriching their hearts. Our words heighten or halt our relationships, so we must choose our words wisely.

Changing the words you say and how you say them changes your outcomes—whether you forgive and are forgiven, whether your relationship makes it or falls apart, whether you're sick or well.

We tend to get caught up in talk that doesn't grow us but grieves us, by talking about what we don't want rather than what we do.

In your relationships with family, friends, and coworkers right now, what if you changed your approach? Instead of saying I don't like this or I don't like that, what if you started saying I prefer this, I prefer that, or I enjoy this? I wonder how much stress and strife that would eliminate.

The power of a marriage relationship is based upon agreement and quality of communication. For example, if a spouse uses negative words to show disapproval, the other spouse will feel apprehensive. Those negative words will set on course a whole chain of events: insecurity will produce fear, then anger, and then withdrawal. The marriage relationship will suffer in intimacy and conversation. One spouse will feel defensive, and the other, frustrated.

But when one spouse says, "I *prefer* when you cook this dish this way because when you do, it's great," or "I *prefer* to go on a walk after dinner," or "I *prefer* that you touch me here," the other receives a lift. These words build confidence because they show appreciation rather than condemnation.

To what extent could our personal relationships and quality of existence be changed by this little verbal tweak?

Call to action

What area is challenging you in a relationship right now?

What are three positive things you could say?

How will this approach affect your relationship?

I think that we don't give a lot of thought to what we speak. When we're rash with our communication, many ramifications come into play, including anxiety, frustration, and fear. It's better to be thoughtful of others and think about what our words are going to produce. To be an effective communicator at any level, put yourself in the other person's shoes. Consider how they think and feel.

Ask yourself, am I really communicating—connecting and getting through? Life is all about dealing with other people, and the key is connecting with them in an effectual way.

If we don't win with the people we come in contact with, we will short-circuit our lives.

We must understand the power of our words. Just as God created the universe and everything in it by his spoken word, we create our personal world and relationships by the words we speak.

Words leave a lasting impression; once we release them into the universe, we can't take them back. Speak some seeds of encouragement. Speak some miracles today into people around you.

Let it go

God tells us to forgive others, but also tells us not to stop there. He instructs us to bless them.

"Bless means" "to speak well of."[3] Using my words to rehash offenses causes me to relapse, but by forgiving and blessing others, I can begin to move forward and enjoy my life with peace.

It's not enough to merely say that we forgive so-and-so. We must be careful to choose our words wisely and not speak evil of people, even if they deserve it. Do what Jesus did to those who wounded him; at the cross—naked, bleeding, dying, and completely exposed before onlookers—he blessed his killers by praying for them: "Father, forgive them" (Luke 23:34). By following his example, we bless not only our offenders, but ourselves.

Why spend your life angry and upset at people who probably don't even know you're angry at them? Those same people have probably moved on and are enjoying their lives while you're still feeling miserable.

It's time to release them. Let the offense go; let it drop. You'll experience freedom and give God a chance to vindicate you.

Relationships often come to an end because of things said and not said. People lose their jobs, cause strife, and embarrass themselves all through the power of their tongue.

Call to action

Don't allow bitterness and a lack of forgiveness to erupt like a volcano inside you, building more tension, more frustration, and a bigger wall. Why don't you stop the fight? Why don't you be the person who rises to the occasion right now? Be the first to forgive and say something nice about someone.

Speak up

At work, as you begin to speak about what can be, you immediately separate yourself from the middle of the pack because most people say, "Here are the limitations, here is the problem, here is the challenge."

Be the first to forgive and say something nice about someone.

Very few people speak up with solutions. Let your mouth be a voice of solution. If you don't have a solution, do your best to hold your tongue. Unlike the law of attraction, you're not partnering with the universe, you're partnering with a personal God. *You can have what you say, if God says it first.* When your voice begins to speak the solutions to problems in your life, it will draw the results you want like a magnet.

Your words will establish your standard of living. Your internal dialog will dictate the tempo of your life. Learn to think and talk about the good life. Don't hinder the good life through retaining old confessions of how you are powerless and unable; instead, talk yourself to the top by saying what God can do.

What are you speaking into existence?

Memory of the future

Instead of remembering negative things that cause worry all day long, remember what God says about your future throughout the day. Develop a memory of the future.

"Have faith in God," Jesus answered. "I tell you the truth, if anyone says to this mountain, 'Go, throw yourself into the sea,' and does not doubt in his heart but believes that what he says will happen, it will be done for him."[4]

Does your mouth rehearse negative events, or does it release you from the past and paint an inviting future? Your faith will lift to the level of your words, and faith-filled words bring God on the scene.

Words really do work—they work for you or against you. The answer is under your nose.

11

Daily Lift

Today, you have twenty-four hours. The question is, what will you do with them?

I want you to enjoy life and find a successful rhythm and approach to your daily routine. You can't change yesterday and you're not yet living in tomorrow, but you have power to operate today. Daily success is all in strategy and the goals you set before you. Today is all about outcome.

Play offense

I went early to a Lakers game and so I started watching the Jumbotron above the floor. They were showing Kobe Bryant, the elite superstar of the NBA as he played defense against a high school basketball superstar at a summer camp. As he dribbled the ball, the high school player began to get very nervous because Kobe Bryant was playing defense against him.

Kobe stopped him and grabbed the ball. He said, "If you play defensively, I will drive you backward, steal the ball from you, and make you look foolish. Get aggressive! Come at me with that ball and put *me* on the defensive."

Watching that I thought, how many of my days am I approaching defensively, letting life hit me so I drift rather than drive my day? How many days do I get out of bed and dread going to the airport, dread having to study, dread having to pray, dread that uncomfortable conversation? I even dread having to do stuff I once loved. I began to realize how dread was slowly sabotaging my enjoyment, causing it to leak out of my life. I realized my life had changed: I was no longer tackling the day aggressively, no longer operating on the offensive to be effective.

Life wants to hit us when we get up. That's when we start thinking of every challenging thing we're going to face that day. Dread sabotages all of our strength, energy, and zest before we even get out of bed.

I've had days where I've woken up and felt tired before my feet even touched the floor because I started thinking about all the responsibilities I had to face that day; all the people I had to talk to, the forty-five messages I had to return on my phone, all the e-mails I had to get to, the studying I had to do to prepare for places I had to go to, the speaking I had to do that night, the couple of projects I had to work on; and, my dog was acting up. On days like that, I haven't felt well and I've thought, I'm already tired and I'm ready to go back to bed; I don't even want to live this day.

I was traveling to a lot of great places, but I couldn't say I was enjoying my life or enjoying the places. I didn't know how to enjoy anything. All that changed by seeing the high schooler take on Kobe on the Jumbotron.

That's when I decided, I'm going to start my day in drive. I'm not going to start my day defensively back paddling, but on the offensive.

I learned through study that I set the nature of my life on course by the words I speak, that my words are carriers of life and death, and that when I speak God's words, he will confirm them with miracles, signs, and wonders.

Knowing this caused me to realize that I wanted to start my day by being thankful and speaking what God in me can do and say—as if God really does live on the inside of me, because I know he does! I knew those words would generate thoughts and emotions and passion inside of me to move me in a direction I wanted to go and would replace my feelings of dread. I knew they would begin to program my mind for change, so I started looking for something to happen!

Instead of starting the day with a negative, conditioned response, I started the day on offense by acknowledging every good thing. That allowed me to be set in drive and expectation—working at an outcome as opposed to waiting to see what would happen during the day. Philemon 1:6 became a reality: my faith became powerful because I acknowledged every good thing that is in me in Christ Jesus.

I began to enjoy life by starting my day with certain things I speak. By speaking these words, I started changing my atmosphere and my mood. As Psalm 45:1 describes, my heart started overflowing with a good theme. The more I began to speak those words, the more energy and rhythm I felt.

The result has been a life marked by miracles. I began to shift the way I look for things to happen in my life—I expected positive events instead of things to go wrong. My days began to feel like treasure hunts!

I have discovered that God's Word needs a voice to change circumstances on the earth. Therefore, I encourage you to set your life on course by activating the divine nature that God has designed for you by speaking in agreement with him about your life!

I personally use a confession list in my own life on a consistent basis, and I believe this one will empower you as it has empowered me:

Thank you for the opportunity of life today. I thank you that good things are going to take place because your favor surrounds me like a shield. I expect increase, promotion, and favorable opportunities to happen all day long. I thank you that because I am your child, all of my needs will be met and that your strength and power will enable me to live above my feelings. Today I choose to walk by faith and not by sight. I declare that I will not be overcome by evil, but I will overcome evil with good. Today I will fear no evil, for you do not give me a spirit of fear, but of power, love, and a sound mind. Today I will set my mind and keep it set on the things of God; therefore I will enjoy a mind that is full of life and peace. Today I am healthy, strong, vibrant, and full of energy. I am a giver, meeting the needs of people around me. I choose to love the Lord with all my heart, mind, body, and strength. I choose to enjoy my life, my work, and the people in my life. Today I will increase in the knowledge of God and I will be strengthened with all might according to his glorious power. I will let the peace of God rule my heart, mind, and nerves and I refuse to worry or be of an anxious mind. Today I will walk in honor and integrity, and I will esteem others better than myself. Today is a day of victory, health, success, opportunity, and miracles. Today is the greatest day of my life!

Jump in some puddles today

During a flood in southern California, in some places the water rose halfway up car doors and in most places caused widespread traffic congestion. I was stuck in gridlock, along with a lot of other people who were noticeably irritated. Driven by pressure to be somewhere, I saw them react by honking and using hand gestures.

To my right, a school was letting out for the day and I watched the children as they exited the building. Laughing, they tossed down their bags, threw off their Uggs and tennis shoes, and jumped in the puddles!

The same weather the adults were angry and cussing about was the very weather the kids were enjoying and splashing around in.

You're not too busy to enjoy your life.

Remember flying kites and chasing the ice cream truck as a kid? It's time to create some happiness in your life again. Psychologists say kids laugh over 150 times a day, but adults laugh only four to eight times a day. I wonder if that's a reason why we're so stressed out. Let's recapture the ability to laugh and enjoy our lives.

It's time to stop approaching life like an old fart and start approaching life like a young kid. Maybe one reason Jesus instructed people to enter God's kingdom like children is because children enjoy life. The kingdom of God is righteousness, peace, and joy in the Holy Spirit.

How can we enjoy life? By choosing to be in a good mood. I think the best way is by choosing to be thankful. It's a decision we make.

Not everything in life is inherently enjoyable, so we have to choose to enjoy it. Choose to enjoy the beginning of projects, the middle of projects, and the end. Choose to enjoy the drive home, even in the midst of traffic. You can dread it, hate it, and let it irritate you or you can choose to be in a good mood and make the most of it. You're going to finish the project and make the drive anyway. Personally, I have hours of driving and flying to speak all over the world, so I've decided I might as well be in a good mood and enjoy my trips, rather than dread them.

When we arrive home after work, we face family responsibilities. Well, we can despise those or we can dispense with the bad feelings and enjoy, appreciate, and gain the value of them.

We tend to say, "When I arrive, then I'm going to enjoy my life...when I make this amount of money, when I have this degree, when I finish this season of my life, when...when... when..." The truth is, we're always going to be headed somewhere because God created us to keep going.

Why put enjoyment of our lives off into the future? There is nothing worse than going through life and hating it.

Let me ask you, are you being driven by pressure or are you being driven by enjoyment? Life should be savored, not just quickly gulped down. Savor your days. You only have one life; you might as well enjoy it.

Take time to enjoy your life! God enjoys creation and creating. He enjoys life.

Action thought:

Today, instead of saying, "I need this situation to change," I will focus on what I do have, and enjoy it.

Thankfulness turns deficiencies into opportunities.

Thankfulness turns deficiencies into opportunities.

Say no

Simplify your day to amplify your results.

So many people own stockpiles of junk. Lives are overwhelmed because people allow things to accumulate. People refuse to say no, they refuse to throw things in the trash can, they refuse to delete e-mails, and they refuse to put away their clothes, so they allow trash to keep piling and piling and piling. People's lives are crowded, and crowding creates stress and irritation, but people continue to get more.

That's what I call stressful increase as opposed to restful increase.

Let's tackle that pile of junk in our lives today. Living on the offensive allows us to eliminate whatever must not dominate our day.

Narrowing your focus expands your reach. Eliminate many things so you can reach your desired outcome.

Simplify for significance. Knowing the purpose of your life simplifies your life; knowing your purpose defines what you say no to and what you say yes to.

Say yes

Own this day; face it head on. When you intentionally order your day, good things unfold in your life. Give your mind to what you're doing.

When you decide what you'll accomplish, you're doing something with your day rather than letting it do something with you. Let's start right now with priorities.

Prioritizing your time makes time work for you, not against you. It allows you to connect with people rather than just casually talk with them, resulting in personal growth.

Prioritizing reduces procrastination. Any time you procrastinate, you're cutting yourself off from moving into your future. When you think of the word "decision," think of the word "incision"—when you decide what you will value today, you will cut things away that steal from an outcome you want.

What things do you need to aggressively tackle today?

Call to action

1. What are three things you've been putting off that will cost you more time, energy, and money if you don't tackle them today?

   These could be things you've dreaded like paying a parking ticket or going to the dentist because you don't like to go and sit there.

2. Who will you call today to say "I appreciate you"?

   By doing this, you're doing more than having a generic relationship; you're connecting with someone today. You're actively valuing someone's life.

And remember, what you sow is what you reap. What you choose to invest in, will appreciate. Quantity is one thing and I'm into having quantity, but I'm more excited about quality in all areas of your life, including relationships with your family and friends.

3. What are two things you will do today to enhance the quality of your physical life? Some ideas are:

Go for a walk

At lunchtime, leave work and go to the gym

Schedule twenty minutes for some Pilates stretches

Eat extra fruits and vegetables

As you exercise and eat better, think about how much you'll improve not only on this day, but how much you'll reduce your stress and overall cholesterol count if you continue four to five days a week over approximately fifty-two weeks this year.

4. You are loaded with unexposed ability and treasure within. What will you do today to grow your gift and skill?

Maybe it's applying to school to take a dance class or to learn a trade, or maybe it's simply one quick step in the right direction.

5. Wouldn't today be a good time to schedule some happiness in your life? When was the last time you got away, or watched a funny movie and laughed?

I don't want you to live your day in neutral, with feelings and thoughts of dread. For an optimum day, get on the offensive and enjoy life!

12

Secret Advantage

Let me tell you the story of a woman named of Kate. I was speaking at a conference in Iowa and we were sitting at a table before the meeting began in the morning. She asked, "May I tell you my story?" I said, "Sure, go ahead."

Kate said, "When I was born, I was labeled mentally retarded." I looked at her, a very together, beautiful woman, and I thought, surely, you're not telling me the truth; this doesn't add up.

She continued, "I was put in the Special Ed classes ever since I was a young child and I heard the taunts of students saying, 'You're retarded! You're slow!'"

I could imagine what she went through because, as a kid, I watched students walk to the slow class and I heard other students saying, "You're retarded," and other hurtful, cruel, and reckless comments.

Growing up, Kate had a passion to play basketball, but her mental disability and retarded label separated her from her desire. She said, "I wasn't allowed to be on the high school team because I was in the Special Ed system."

One summer evening, her grandmother took her to an event where she heard about God's favor. After that, she adopted this scripture: "For You, O Lord, will bless the righteous; with favor You will surround him as with a shield" (Ps. 5:12).

She said, "From that moment, I began to picture a shield of God's favor around me. I started picturing myself favored."

Walking to her Special Ed classes, she still heard the taunts, but she kept saying, "The favor of God surrounds me like a shield. The favor of God is going to make me smarter. I'm going to play basketball. God's favor is going to make a way where there is no way."

Here's the rest of the story. When Kate graduated from high school, she graduated as the valedictorian of her class, and received top basketball honors for being the top scorer in her state that year.

How could someone go from mentally retarded to valedictorian? Favor. How could someone go from not making the team to leading scorer? Favor.

How can you go from where you are today to where you dream of? Favor.

What if you tapped into the favor of God for your life? It's available to you as you become more aware of it, so decide to become more favor-minded. Expect God's supernatural assistance and special advantage to lift you out of things that are limiting you and place you into things that release the best you.

Another way you can access it is by declaring and confessing God's favor in your life. You might say things like, "God, I thank you that I have your favor and that your favor is opening doors of opportunity and bringing success into my life. Thank you that your favor is causing people to want to help me; therefore, I will expect good things to happen today."

Call to action

It's interesting that the favor of God recorded in the Bible caused people such as Esther, Ruth, and Daniel to live above their means and gave them incredible meaning. Do you see yourself beyond where you are financially, emotionally, relationally, in your sex life, in your spiritual life?

If I were coaching you, I would ask you to create room in your mind to see yourself three times beyond where you are now. This is important to do because, many times, your concept of who you are and where you can go determines where you show up and what comes your way.

Air Force One

Hearing Kate talk about declaring God's favor over her life caused me to shift what I said about my life. At that point, I had spoken a lot about what is, and not about what will be through God's favor. Her story elevated my level of expectation, and I was amazed how God met me at my new level of communication as soon as I started it.

Only a couple of days after hearing Kate's story, I was invited to Los Angeles International Airport to witness President Bush's Air Force One arrive. I was excited to be included in that little gated community on the tarmac that would watch him and his entourage get off the plane.

As I arrived at the airport and got my pass, I realized I didn't have a special pass to get on the airplane. I thought, oh man, I got all the way here just to watch him get off the airplane and into his limo and bounce. Then I thought, wait a second; I'm missing something here! I began to recall how Kate spoke God's favor into existence, and that God's Word always needs a voice. The question was, would I give voice to it? I decided to start that day, right there.

I just started declaring out loud, "God's favor surrounds my life like a shield!"

A couple of Hollywood entertainers from a hit TV show were with me, but I just started declaring out loud, "God's favor surrounds my life like a shield!"

One of them said, "Shut up, Rex. You're making a scene."

I said, "No, I have to try this. If I don't take a shot at getting on that airplane, I'm going to regret not doing this. Who cares if anyone thinks I'm weird?" So again, I said, "God's favor surrounds me like a shield. God's going to hook me up. I'm going to get the best there is to offer. There is going to be a way for me to get on that plane. God's favor is going to make a way for me."

Now both of them said, "Rex, you're making a scene!"

Well, a pilot from Air Force One walked over from the plane to me. She said, "Do you have a pass to get on the airplane?"

I said, "No, but I'm favored."

I'm sure she thought, are you okay? do you need your medication? But she said, "Would you like to get on that airplane? Let me see what I can do for you."

I said, "Okay."

She went back on the plane, and all the while my friends were saying to me, "Maybe this is going to work out! Maybe this is going to work out!" My level of communication shifted to them and they began to expect something to change.

Later, the lady pilot returned, after the seventeen people with special passes had finished their tours. She said, "We have never allowed this before, but I'm so excited to say, we can bring you aboard now that everyone else is done with their tours." She introduced us to our tour guides, and they took us first to President Bush's bedroom.

When they took me into his room, I got to sit on his bed, and let me tell you something! I didn't just sit still and say, "Wow, this is great!" Heck no, I was bouncing on that bed saying the favor of God hooked me up.

From there, they took us to the airplane's hospital operating room. Then they said, "We've never done this for any other civilian guests—we would like to take you to the cockpit."

Walking into the cockpit was the most amazing, exhilarating feeling! Then, sitting there on top of the tarmac, gripping the steering wheel of Air Force One, I started saying out loud, "God, your favor is better than life. I don't deserve this, but thank you so much for it."

Air Force One tours are twenty minutes long, but two hours and twenty minutes later, we left the plane. As we departed, the flight attendants lavished us with gifts and some of the china that had been used on Air Force One. They asked, "May we take a picture with you?

They gave us the royal treatment. We left an atmosphere that was overwhelmingly full of life and full of goodness.

May I tell you, all of that experience was set on course because I started saying, "The favor of God surrounds my life like a shield."

I wonder...What would happen if you truly bought into the concept that God's unmerited favor surrounds your life? What could begin to take place as you anticipate God's power and kindness to move in your job, finances, health, and relationships? I have confidence that it would look something like this: promotion, financial increase, physical healing, internal breakthroughs, and quality relationships.

Favor silences failure

The preferential treatment of God exists to enable you.

You might not have a Nike deal worth one hundred million dollars like Lebron James, but you have an endorsement deal with Jehovah, the supreme God who is for you and who backs you up. If I were you, I'd accept that over any other endorsement deal any day of the week because then I'd know I couldn't fail.

Think for just a moment: Are you accepting and expecting God's favor in your life?

Don't let insecurity and doubt silence the voice of God that wants to open you up to his favor. Let favor silence the voice of failure in your life.

God has your back.

13

Relationships

In your busy life, have you found time to live with real meaning? I'm not talking about just closing the big deal, or having a couple kids, or purchasing the home of your dreams. While all of that is wonderful and I pray that you have all that and more, I'm more interested in this: Have you learned to love?

As a society, we've become busy bodies—overwhelmed and overworked with overcrowded schedules—who just try to fit love in. But in reality, nothing apart from love really matters. Love should be our greatest aim and our greatest pleasure.

I've discovered that life is about relationships: one we have with God, one we have with ourselves, and one we share with people we live and work with every day. Relationships are what life is all about.

LIFE *Lift*

Loving God

Of all the relationships in your life, the most important one is your relationship with God.

Love and relationships start and begin with him, for love is who he is, not just something he gives. Before you were born, he designed you out of love. That's right—even if you were born through an adverse circumstance or to a parent who didn't want you or plan you, God planned you. You are not some mass-produced or manufactured idea, but deliberately selected and precisely put together. Every person is a brand-new idea from the mind of God.

Over the last fourteen years of traveling the world, I've seen how religion has destroyed the hearts of millions, leaving them longing for the love only God can freely give. Religious systems have come up with ritualistic activities to try to obtain God's love, yet when people complete those duties, they're left with a bigger hole of disappointment and a growing emptiness in their hearts. Does this describe your experience?

We all need to ask ourselves, what am I doing with the love God has for me? Are we accepting and receiving it by faith or are we rejecting it because we don't feel we're worth loving? It's important to begin here, because if we don't receive God's love, we won't be able to love ourselves or others properly.

God's greatest pleasure is to be believed and his worst pain is to be disbelieved. How would you like to overhear your children telling their friends, "My mom and dad lie to me all the time. I just don't believe anything they say." You would be crushed! The same with God.

Think about it for a minute: You exist simply because he wills you to exist. Since you were made by him and for him, living disconnected from him will leave you feeling dissatisfied.

Isn't a relationship with God what you truly desire—a relationship with someone who can see all that's good and bad about you and still love you unconditionally?

Let me offer further insight to help and empower you: It's a part of God's character to think well of you.

God told a man by the name of Jeremiah, "I know the thoughts and plans that I have for you..." Stop right there. How interesting is that? God thinks about us.

It's a part of God's character to think well of you.

I wonder what he's thinking. Well, according to him, "...thoughts and plans for welfare and peace and not for evil, to give you hope in your final outcome."[1]

God sees your whole reality and says, "I love you, I want you, and I'm only interested in doing you good." He knows you don't do everything right; that's why he sent Jesus to reconcile you to himself so you could receive his love and he could love you affectionately.

Maybe you've never experienced his love before. His love will forgive your sins and your past, will give you a new opportunity at life, and will cause your spirit to become alive again. All you have to do is believe.

His love is kind, and not impatient. His love is willing to relate to you right where you are. His love will allow you to experience peace in your heart and mind and remove the fear that has troubled and tormented you.

I've shared this truth with over thirty million people over the years, from the up-and-comers in New York City to the down-and-outers on the streets in Africa. I've watched people open their hearts to God's love, bringing them freedom and giving them a new meaning and a new mission in life—to love.

I'm curious, what is your concept of God?

I'm curious, what is your concept of God? Is he kind and forgiving? Or is he stingy, easily angered, and mean?

Developing a relationship with God isn't hard. Talk to him and allow him to speak to you from the Bible. Biblical words are his words to you, to nourish your heart with faith, peace, and wisdom. His wisdom will allow you to discover the power and grace of God in your life. True love, peace, and joy come from a relationship with your maker. People search for love and happiness through successful and exciting jobs, money, relationships, food, sex, and drugs. Personally, I've tried them all and so have countless others.

Here's how you get there: The Bible says, "Draw near to God, and He will draw near to you."[2] Take a moment and pray; become definite with the infinite. Jesus said it best: "Ask, and you will receive, that your joy may be full."[3]

Loving Yourself

It's amazing how tough we are on ourselves. We beat ourselves up so much that we start believing we're not worth loving and appreciating. Many social and emotional problems stem from the fact that most people really don't like themselves. They are uncomfortable with how they look, how they talk, and how they act. Therefore, they live wishing they had someone else's life, personality, and job.

Are you constantly feeling bad and uncertain about yourself?

An epidemic of insecurity runs rampant in our world today, causing people to feel uncertain and bad about themselves. It steals their sense of joy and causes major problems in their relationships.

All of us long for a sense of security. Security enables us to enjoy healthy thinking and healthy living. Security makes us feel safe, accepted, and approved of.

I went through a tough season years ago that shook the foundation of my security; I found myself getting a divorce. This was a circumstance I thought I'd never go through; somehow, I believed divorce wasn't possible in my life. In the midst of this experience, I felt very alone, even when I was speaking to cheering crowds. Often afterward, I'd get in my car feeling confused and hurt. I no longer liked who I was because I'd listened to so many condemning thoughts replaying in my mind about how awful I was. I kept wondering how someone like me could be going through something like this. The thoughts and feelings of failure began to unravel and defeat me. At one point, I even began to think about how I'd like to get off this planet to escape the pain.

I knew God loved me, but the problem was, I wasn't receiving God's love personally. Therefore, I wasn't able to love myself. It was as if my failure was holding me hostage.

As I got into my car one night after speaking to a packed-out auditorium where God had touched people's lives, I looked into the mirror and asked God to tell me something nice about myself.

His answer surprised me. I felt as though he urged me to go home, look in the mirror, and say some positive things about myself that he said about me in the Bible. For sure, I felt a little dumb; yet, I felt I had nothing to lose.

Back home, I looked in the mirror and began to confess, "You're wonderfully made, Rex; God still loves you and approves of you, Rex; God will restore your soul and your fortune before your eyes. Your future will be better than your past."

As I kept saying this, confidence began to emerge from somewhere deep within, and clouds of depression slowly started parting. I felt the courage to forgive myself and to begin the journey of loving myself again.

Looking back, I think I got caught in a familiar cycle that I've encountered in people just about everywhere I go. It's a sick cycle of loving ourselves when we perform, yet not enjoying ourselves otherwise.

Any relationship that is unrecognized will become uncelebrated, including the one we have with ourselves. When I started acknowledging who God made me to be, I started feeling good about myself. A new sense of confidence, joy, and celebration replaced insecurity and inferiority.

If you see yourself through the lenses of weakness and failure long enough, you'll hinder not only your relationship with yourself, but your relationship with others. We all have room to grow, and personal change will come as we learn to like and appreciate ourselves.

Rejecting ourselves doesn't change us; actually, it complicates and cripples our lives. People who reject themselves do so because they don't see themselves in a right way. They see themselves through eyes of failure, or as someone who is unlovable and unacceptable. In Psalm 139, King David raves about how wonderfully God made him. Don't ever say another negative word about yourself. Instead, speak words over your life that will empower you and put you over, not under.

Your relationships with others will reflect the way you love yourself. You cannot enjoy and appreciate someone else until you learn to love and appreciate who you are. Nine times in the Bible, God says you shall love your neighbor as yourself. If he stresses it that many times, we can be sure it's highly important to pay attention to. I find it interesting that he emphasizes love for ourselves as well as for our neighbor.

Your relationships with others will reflect the way you love yourself.

Your uniqueness and individual personality mixed with your gift and talents make you a wonder. Decide to love and appreciate who you are!

Call to action

What five words best describe who you think you are?

What five words best describe who God thinks you are?

LIFE *Lift*

Loving Others

I wonder who needs your love today—your smile, encouraging words, or listening ear—for just a few minutes? If we took counsel from the famous love chapter, we would find that the basic ingredients of love are patience and kindness.[4] Patience is a response to someone and kindness is an action toward someone, so it's interesting that love is both reactive and active. These two ingredients dramatically help us improve our relationships with others.

A friend of mine named Jennifer is an exceptional speaker and author, and she told me a very enriching story. She said that every morning, whether she's at home in Las Vegas or speaking in another city, she goes to Starbucks. One day, she decided to pay in advance for the person's drink behind her. She made this a habit, practicing the principle of reaping what you sow. Out of town one morning, she went to the counter, and as usual, started to pay for the person's drink behind her. When she did, the cashier asked her, "Why did you do that? Are you *her*?"

Jennifer was puzzled.

"Are you the woman from Las Vegas?"

Jennifer identified herself, and the cashier explained that Starbucks had highlighted her in their newsletter. The newsletter said, because of Jennifer's generosity, one morning over one hundred people followed her example.

Jennifer's kind routine influenced others to give, too. She has forever messed up Starbucks in a good way because of her choice to invest in a stranger's day in a simple, kind way.

Patience is the second ingredient that dramatically helps us improve our relationships with ourselves and others. We've all heard "patience is a virtue," but let me frame it for you another way: Cut people some slack.

People are usually trying their best. By being patient, you will enjoy life and appreciate people a lot more. You'll enjoy your ride to work rather than letting it bother you. You'll appreciate time with your kids rather than wish you were doing something different.

Taking time to love

Saying "I love you" is worthless without action.

Loving others takes time and effort, but think of the rewards to be gained by giving yourself to a life of loving others. Investing in others brings eternal value to your life. Making people your highest value creates the life of your dreams. Give your life away, and find that people will rally around you when you need them the most.

What we value, we make time for. We need to give the gift of our presence. Our presents only take us so far; what people need is us. When we give ourselves, we make a sacrifice, and sacrifice is the essence of love. Loving someone is choosing to give up our comfort, time, and energy for their benefit. Relational investment is worth more than the risk.

Go beyond acknowledging people with a smile—treat them with dignity and honor. Without love, everything else is a waste, so refuse to waste another day.

Action thought:

It's time to make my life count by showing a patient attitude and a kind approach toward every person I come into contact with today.

Call to action

When you wake up in the morning, why not get on the offensive by thinking about who you will love? By loving God and others, you'll set up your day to be lived with meaning and purpose.

- What if you begin with God? Don't frustrate yourself by forgetting to invite him on the journey of your day. How could you show him some love and thanksgiving? Maybe by writing him a note of appreciation for all he has done for you.

- Then, what about somebody in your family? It might be your wife or husband, child, or parent who needs an extra hug or call from you.

- What is the name of someone else who needs your love in a special way today? What will you do?

Improving relationships through transparency and vision

The play *The Phantom of the Opera* depicts the wrong way to improve a relationship. Wanting to be loved, the phantom subverts his true talents, puts on a mask, and lives in the underworld, trying to engage people through tricks, loud organ music, smoke, and other negative special effects. The result?

People are afraid of him. Only when his mask is ripped off does he receive an honest kiss from his love, Christine.

Like the phantom, do you wear a mask or have you learned to be transparent? When we're totally open, true love and learning can originate. Jesus, the master of life, revealed not only his plans and power to those closest to him, but also his longings and heartaches.

Don't write off your family, friends, coworkers, and neighbors because of your familiarity with their weaknesses and habits. Be open to their ideas—not all great ideas have to come from you—and they earnestly desire to be believed in and will flourish when somebody truly does.

Give your relationships a fresh vision. People crave something larger than themselves, so where there is no vision, our relationships lose their passion and their power. When our relationships shift in focus from mere survival to something beyond, energy and excitement are released, bringing greater pleasure and purpose.

Vision releases new energy to take our relationships into a new tomorrow. Revisit what brought your relationships together and reinforce what that person or persons mean to you. This will allow a greater emotional bond, releasing new vision, new energy, and passion.

Ask God to give you a vision of the value and significance each person's life holds, and then become the voice that calls that out. God placed seeds of greatness in everyone, and usually, all that greatness needs for release is someone to call it out.

For the past twenty years, a friend and mentor of mine has been a voice that has released the unseen and untapped potential I didn't see in myself. I've watched how this man lives, and it's interesting to me that people are drawn to him like a magnet. I've noticed he's always smiling and telling people around him something good and positive about themselves. He told me that it's tough to be in a bad mood when he's constantly lifting people up and speaking to what they can do. I've watched how that practical approach enriches his life in the quantity and quality of his personal relationships. People always want him around because he's always dispensing empowering words. In turn, opportunities chase him down from every direction.

In our relationships, do we give people an experience that is forgettable or memorable? Do we fuel people or infuriate them? Produce faith or fear? Give pain or pleasure?

Action thought:
Whose value will I call out today?

Givers and takers

We've already learned that the only way our relationships will work effectively is to look at them as a place to give. We know that we must cultivate them, which involves sacrifice, time, and energy; and, that we must care for them, which means nourishing them with kindness and patience.

Therefore, before getting personally involved with someone, the question we should ask ourselves is, am I entering this relationship to get something or give something? Consider this: Am I getting into this relationship because I want this person to make me feel good?

Concerning existing relationships, we should ask ourselves a different question: Is this relationship a place where I'm celebrated or tolerated?

How long will you keep pleasing a "friend" at your own expense? Refuse to live in fear of someone like that—pleasing that person wastes the time you could spend with someone who celebrates you.

Your answers to these questions will determine the destiny of both old and new relationships.

From criticism to compliments

Do you believe the best of the people closest to you, such as your wife, husband, or children? Criticism and condemnation will not bring out the best in them.

When we hold on to hurts and grudges and become cynical and sarcastic toward someone, strife gains ground, melting away patience and kindness. Forgiveness is a choice and a process, so continue to forgive until you can think of your loved one without any ill feelings.

Learn to encourage the people around you by complimenting them.

Learn to encourage the people around you by complimenting them; your children, your coworkers, and your family all need your compliments. If you tell them they're bad, average, or dysfunctional, that's what you'll get out of them. Instead, speak to them of the way you want them to act.

Look for ways to deepen your emotional connection with those you love. Reassessing what you love and enjoy about them reinforces your bond.

Even if currently in a mess, you can give a relationship renewed meaning by (1) thinking about what that person has invested in you, (2) recalling shared moments, and (3) vocalizing ways they've enriched your life.

Talking and then talking some more together achieves peace and common ground. Compliments are a powerful way to come together and stay together. While complaints separate us, compliments unite us. Compliments change the atmosphere from hostile to happy. For example, tell your spouse, "How did I get so lucky to have you?"

Learn to appreciate who God designed your loved ones to be. Instead of trying to change them, make loving deposits that help them feel better and become better people.

Action thought:
How can I give a loved one confidence to succeed?

Exposing weaknesses

The reality is, we're all different.

It's easy to become offended because we don't always see eye to eye. We must realize, every one of us has weaknesses coupled with strengths, and love makes allowances for people's mistakes and weaknesses.

Love covers weaknesses instead of exposing them.

One of God's friends messed up one night and drank too much, leaving him in a drunken state. Inside his tent, his body became uncovered, revealing his nakedness. When one of his sons saw him, he went and told on him, but his other two sons discreetly covered him up.[5]

What about you? Are you one who's good at covering the weakness in another, or are you one who points out the weakness and exploits it?

If some of your relationships are diving rather than thriving, exposing the weaknesses of others could be the reason. For you to be successful in relationships, you need to begin to overlook some things. Refuse to flaunt someone else's failures.

Always remember, relationships without mercy are full of misery. One of love's major ingredients is keeping no record of wrongs.

Action thought:

Whose weaknesses am I currently keeping a record of?

Deathbed request

Love is indeed the main objective of our lives, for if we miss out on love, we have truly missed out on life. On their deathbed, I have never heard of people asking for their Armani suit or their Oscar. Quite the opposite! People want to see those they've shared the moments of life with; those they've loved and enjoyed.

Loving people is the greatest impact we can make and leave on this planet. It's love that makes memories and truly leaves a legacy. Refuse to wait till it's too late to realize that relationships are what life is about.

Make relationships your top priority.

14

Partnerships and Toxic Relationships

We were designed to live and work together. Our efforts and endeavors together produce more fruit and better results than flying solo.

Partners are people who unite us with our tomorrows through common goals. Partners are "can people."

Can people are enriching. Can people are those who (1) find opportunities, (2) feed on impossibilities, and (3) focus on how they can do them.

Deal or no deal

Partnership checklist:

✔ "Can two people walk together without agreeing on the direction?" (Amos 3:3 NLT). *Two cannot partner together unless they agree.*

✔ "Two are better than one, because they have a good reward for their labor. For if they fall, one will lift up his companion. But woe to him who is alone when he falls, for he has no one to help him up...Though one may be overpowered by another, two can withstand him" (Eccl. 4:9-10, 12). *Two are better than one; partnership has power.*

✔ "A friend loves at all times, and a brother is born for adversity" (Prov. 17:17).

✔ "He who walks with wise men will be wise, but the companion of fools will be destroyed" (Prov. 13:20).

Jesus called Matthew from his position as a tax collector to a disciple. Partners carry us from our impossibility to our breakthrough. Their faith helps pull us through.

Dreamers, doubters, deceivers

Dreamers are fit to be your partners because they help bring your future into focus. They stir up and strengthen your passion and plans by the words they speak and the assistance they offer. These are the ones who add fuel to the engine of your heart. When you're with them, time escapes too fast. You think, where did the last three hours go?

Doubters are full of pessimism that drains you of your desire to try something new. They are "can't people."

Can't people are those who (1) resist opportunities, (2) rehearse impossibilities, and (3) reject the personal cost of getting involved.

Partnerships with can't people are foolish entanglements. Avoid can't people because they'll set you up for failure on both a personal and a professional level.

Doubters are people who like you and might even love you, but they devalue your dreams through their doubts, suspicions, and dreadful outlook. When you describe a dream that lacks a predictable return or that's a big undertaking, doubters point out why it can't happen rather than why it can. Known for the constant drama they add to your life, they are the ones who are always speaking about tough times, negative current events, and why things will never change. They're famous for phrases such as, "you can't, probably not, and I'm not sure."

Doubters aren't fit to partner with you because they don't share a passion for your purpose.

Doubters aren't fit to partner with you because they don't share a passion for your purpose. They are takers, not givers. And when it comes to your personal relationships, these relational consumers can become lethal.

Deceivers are those who disguise themselves as your friends and partners, but you find out later, they were only in the relationship to exploit and exhaust you. Like clever thieves, they are takers whose whole bent is how much they can get from you. After they use you for their own purposes, they leave you robbed of the love you gave which they never returned. You're left with loss and harm to reputation, potential, or property.

Like wolves in sheeps' clothing, they mislead and betray you. They know how to smooth-talk you out of God's plan and into theirs where you compromise who you are. Deceivers are false friends who lead you to believe they have your best interest in mind, when you're not on their minds at all. They smile, but their charm is deceptive.

Action thought:

Who will I partner with? What do they bring to the table?

Toxic people

I was at dinner with a company owner who was about to put on an event for over eight thousand people. I knew from his past engagements that he would bring in a great musical guest to entertain and engage the crowd, so I casually brought up the idea of bringing in an artist I'd had the privilege to help over the past years.

As I said the artist's name, I was excited to hear the owner say he'd heard of him and really enjoyed his music. He went on to tell me that he thought the artist would be such a great fit, he would call his people right then and there. I was excited for them!

Just when I thought I'd hear the good news they'd worked out a deal, the conversation took a downward spiral. After he hung up, the company owner told me the artist's manager started demanding so much money and so many luxuries that he finally said, "I don't think we have the same mind-set."

This well-off gentleman would have taken care of the artist with over-and-above kindness and compensation. Yet, because of his manager's pushy side, he decided not to book him.

An interesting part of this story is that I had spoken with this artist over ten times during that past year about being wise about who he allowed to represent him. I'd shown him the liabilities of his current managerial relationship on paper. He had responded, "I see this isn't good for me, so I'm going to remove him." Over the last year, I'd kept hearing him say he was going to switch that partnership, but then he would talk about how badly he felt for the manager because of some personal issues.

The businessman offered him a fantastic opportunity, but he didn't know about it or have a choice about it, all because the person he chose to represent him sabotaged the opportunity with bad business ethics. As I left the table that night, I picked up my cell phone to let him know he would've had a bigger deal than he'd wanted, but because of the pushy, prima donna attitude of his representative, the company chief wanted nothing to do with him.

This artist's relationship with the person who represented his interest undermined, weakened, and wasted his opportunities, not only in this instance, but as I later learned, in other ventures that had offered him massive opportunity.

The relationships we embrace have such a strong say in who we become, what we experience, and what we achieve!

The sad reality is, not all relationships are beneficial and life giving. While some relationships add, others subtract; while some empower and strengthen us, others should be avoided altogether due to their toxic nature.

Toxic relationships are the ones that weaken our focus and sap our energy. These relationships full of strife and conflict should be avoided or abandoned. If we don't let go, the energy we need to accomplish and become will be consumed by constant conflict.

Toxic people full of strife

Some toxic people are the kind who poison your path with nitpicking and negativity. They are the chronic whiners who take great pleasure in dumping their negative garbage all over you. Cynicism is their chronic conversation, telling you why you can't do this and why you can't become what you actually can. They are specialists in bursting the bubble of hope and positivity in you.

These toxic people are chronic complainers who eventually no longer increase you. They are predators instead of partners.

Sever their ties of strife and suspicion that strangle you.

Action thoughts:

Are my relationships full of constant disagreement? Am I spending my time defending myself to people who just don't get me?

Toxic people who keep me in my then

Abraham went through this experience.

In the Bible, there's a story about God's plans to take Abraham beyond what he'd experienced into a richer, fuller life. Yet, the Bible reveals that God couldn't take him to this new place until he let go of the relationships that were holding him back. When Abraham embraced God's Word to him to leave them, God began to show him the expansion that was coming his way.[1]

Sometimes it's the old relationships that hold us back the most from developing and releasing our potential. Sad to say, out of convenience and comfort we tend to hold on to relationships where the only thing we have in common is our past. These toxic relationships keep us looking backwards. They're the ones where we constantly talk and revisit old memories of what once was; the ones where we constantly stroll down memory lane about the things we used to do and places we used to go. While these wonderful memories make us smile, if these are all we share in common, then these relationships are anchoring us to our then when we are living in our now.

Sometimes it's the old relationships that hold us back the most from developing and releasing our potential.

God wants to do some new things that the old can't contain. To move where God wants us to go, we have to be ready to adjust to something new, and so do the people around us, or we can't go there together.

The potential that Jesus carried of doing miracles was hindered in his hometown by the limited vision of people who knew him as a boy. When Jesus returned there to preach in the synagogue, "everyone was amazed and said, 'Where does he get this wisdom and the power to do miracles?' Then they scoffed, 'He's just the carpenter's son'...and they were deeply offended and refused to believe in him...so he did only a few miracles there because of their unbelief."[2]

His former neighbors only knew him according to his then, back when he was working in the carpentry shop, living like everybody else. When he broke out of that into the power of God's purpose for his life, which was to save humanity, he wanted to accomplish more for these people, but their lack of vision and faith in who he was hindered his ability.

All they could see was the carpenter and not the Messiah. They did not and would not look beyond the limited lenses they saw him through, therefore paralyzing his power.

We, too, have people who paralyze our power. These toxic relationships hold back our abilities because they define us on the basis of who we used to be and not who we've become. When these relationships are close to us, they minimize our momentum and keep us from the future we envision.

God has big things ordered for your life that will enlarge and enrich you, but if you fail to cut off the relationships that only honor your past, you will never be in position to see and embrace the new things your future holds.

Action thought:

Thinking of my five closest friends, do any of these alliances anchor me to a limited life?

Toxic forced relationships

The relationships we force our way into so that we can "be somebody" end up costing us dearly. These relationships very often exploit us because, in our eagerness to be included in a certain circle, we allow the plans and priorities of others to extinguish ours.

In reality, all of this happens as a result of our own insecurity, which causes us to think that being in with certain people heightens our value. We exhaust ourselves competing to maintain these relationships, not realizing they're lethal to our potential and quality of life.

Refuse these one-sided relationships. Don't walk anywhere with people who share no passion about what you're going to do *together*.

Relationship detox

When a person detoxifies their body and mind, they are going through a process to remove a poison and free themselves from dependence on it. I've seen many go into a detox program to clean their system from the effect of drugs or alcohol and break the cycle of their dependence on these chemicals. This is a commendable and challenging thing to embrace and the reality is, they gain sobriety, freedom, peace, clarity, and a new chance at life.

Relationally, if we're ever to move beyond where we've been and what we've known, detoxification is a must. Through this process, we will be able to see which relationships multiply and which ones divide our lives.

Remove relationships that weaken your focus, expend your energy, and find fault with what your heart truly wants to be about. To remove a relationship, take stock of it: when you realize the quality of the relationship

Remove relationships that weaken your focus, expend your energy, and find fault with what your heart truly wants to be about.

has shifted, don't divulge as much information or spend as much time with that person. That way, you will conserve your energy for people who are going in your direction. Of course, this doesn't give license to ditch your spouse and family members.

Relationship lift

Love is kind. It looks for a way to be constructive and improve someone else. Through partnering with the right people, we will multiply the difference we make in the lives of people who need our love and encouragement.

Take time to make a difference. Think and plan how, together, you can make someone else's life better today.

There is no greater investment in life than building people.

15

Hero

One Sunday underneath a tent in Kenya, I met a beautiful black child. He had no mother and father because both had died because of AIDS. He was four years old, but was the size of a nine- to ten-month-old. His name was Bonafus.

The people who brought him to me said he didn't walk or talk, and I noticed the effects of an infirmity in his skin tone. His medical records showed that he had been hospitalized about every other week since birth with the immune deficiency he'd been born with—full-blown AIDS. As a result, he quickly caught any virus in the atmosphere. His face and body reflected the effects of the disease because his immune system was too weakened and depleted to outmatch AIDS.

In front of me were masses of people I'd been speaking to about lifting their lives to another level. Now they watched as I greeted this young man. What I didn't know about many people in the African culture was that they will say they love homeless, abandoned kids who have AIDS, but they refuse to touch and embrace them; they won't love that kind of child. This is sad, because there's no better way to demonstrate the reality of love to someone who seems unlovable than through touch.

I think that's what Jesus personified when he healed a man of leprosy. Before he ever healed him, he touched him. He put value and honor and significance on a person everyone else despised.

I'm going to imitate God.

So I took Bonafus in my arms and I held him in front of all the people. I began to walk across the floor and I thought, I can't pull this disease off this child—I don't have the ability—but God always changes people's environments through words, so I'm going to imitate God.

I began to kiss Bonafus profusely, probably to the point of drooling on him. As I did, the Africans were stunned. They stared at me as if to say, "Why would you do that? You're going to make yourself unclean, you're going to make yourself dirty. You just lowered your rank."

I don't think we can lower our rank. I think the greatest thing in the world that we can do is identify with somebody who is suffering, and in this way, put value and honor and significance upon their life.

As I kissed him, I walked and talked to him in front of that crowd of people. I said, "You know what? You are wonderfully made. You are a miracle that's in motion and your greatest days are before you." I even said, "One day, I'm going to take you to Disneyland. You're not going to die, you're going to live. You're not going to die, you're going to live. You're not going to die, you're going to live. You are not going to die as a victim of AIDS, you are going to live. You are not going to die, you are going to live. Even as I'm holding you right now, God's power is flowing through your body. Your blood is being uncontaminated with that virus. God's life is going to flow into your blood, flow into your organs, flow into your limbs, flow into your mind, flow into the neurons of your brain. God's life is going to produce in you, and you will never be the same." As I began to speak, I could feel the presence of God begin to move through the tent. I then handed the boy back to the people who brought him.

After the meeting, I left for two days to go on a safari adventure in Tanzania, and upon my return, I joined Heart for Africa in a big event where we gave orphaned children with AIDS the birthday party they'd never had.

We dressed them as kings and queens and superheroes. They participated in many arts and crafts, played many games, and heard many stories! They were even part of a story about royalty.

While I was there, I was holding Bonafus and putting stickers on his forehead. He was dressed like Spiderman and he had cake all over the side of his face. I saw a little glimmer of a smile, and that's all I could get out of him. Thinking back, I realize it probably hurt him to smile.

A truck pulled up and a group of doctors got out. They said, "Are you Rex Crain? May we speak with you?" We went into a room and sat down. They said, "What did you do to the boy?"

I said, "I don't know what you're talking about."

"What did you do to the boy?"

Again, I said, "I don't know what you're talking about."

They said, "Bonafus, the boy. What did you do to Bonafus?"

I said, "I prayed for him the other day because I was told he had AIDS. What happened?"

"We took him on Monday for a checkup because he'd been having so many complications. We ran four tests for HIV and AIDS and every test came back negative. This happened at a local level, so then we took him for two days to the head hospital of Kenya—the big University Hospital—and their tests yielded the same results."

"I had no idea," I said. "I've been in Tanzania. All I did was call upon the name of my God. His name is Jesus. I started speaking his words of life over the child and commanding his words to manifest in the child's life because I believe you can decree a thing and it will come to pass just as God says it will."

They said, "There isn't a trace of disease in that boy's body."

Miracles are always in motion and God just needs our words to pull them down into the natural world.

When I arrived the following Sunday to speak under the tent again, I saw a little boy in a brand-new Oshkosh outfit chewing a big ole wad of fat green gum. I walked to the front and picked him up in my arms.

I remember hearing people around us singing songs about God, but all I thought about as I held that little boy was that I was holding a miracle. That little boy who couldn't walk, couldn't talk, who had no family, and who almost died, was chewing gum and playing with my lips nonstop. I didn't even care if his germs got in my mouth; I was thinking, miracles are always in motion and God just needs our words to pull them down into the natural world.

From the heart

If you're in a setback right now, be like Katrina. Here is her story:

Several years ago, I was diagnosed with a rare heart disease. Never before had I experienced adverse health symptoms. Over the course of three years, this disease rapidly grew, ravaging my aortic root and aortic valve. When my aortic root was on the verge of bursting, I was told I would need open heart surgery—pronto—and that I could die if I didn't consent to it. However, my heart disease was so rare, the surgery itself called the Bentall procedure was high risk and capable of ending my life. Either way, death could well be the outcome I was facing.

Although this news came as a shock to me, I decided to trust in my heavenly Father, no matter what. I focused on the fact that, though my natural heart was fading, my spiritual heart was alive and strong in Jesus.

When I was initially diagnosed with heart disease, I believed for an instant miracle without surgery. I believe God heals this way, but I learned it takes more faith to walk through something than to receive an instant healing. I had to trust even when I didn't have the answers to all the whys. Of all the ministers who prayed for me, Rex was the only one who said it was okay to go through heart surgery. He assured me that God would be with me, while the other ministers condemned me, saying I didn't have enough faith for a miracle! (Not true! God heals in different ways.)

On a sunny April day, I was sitting on the stretcher in my hospital room, waiting to be wheeled into the operating room. I couldn't help but be incredibly thankful that I had faith in God. My thoughts drifted back to the previous night when I had declined to take the sleeping pills the doctors had offered me (something they often do to alleviate a patient's stress the night before surgery). I'd declined on the simple fact that I had read my Bible for encouragement and prayed to Jesus like I always had. These acts resulted in a peace that reached beyond my understanding. They calmed my soul and gave me inner strength. I knew the creator of the universe had my life in his hands. The peace stayed for a remarkably long time; so long, that it overcame my biggest fear: What if I die during surgery? With my fears wiped away, I became okay with death. Truly, the grace and strength I received from the living God overcame my fear. I received inner peace that was deeper than my own measly courage.

Prior to my surgery date, I was the one who was encouraging those around me, professing that God was taking care of me. I even wrote my family a letter describing the strength and peace I experienced leading up to my big day, and I left it for them in my coat pocket at the hospital the day of my surgery. When someone came to wheel me into the OR, I told my parents about it and encouraged them to read it. When they did, they knew God had given me a strength that reached further than a human soul could grasp. They knew it was the grace of God.

The OR was quite intense, with massive medical machinery and nurses and doctors running around in scrubs. I was instructed to lie myself down on the OR table. I felt an inkling of fear, but I brought my thoughts back to the deep trust I have in knowing God. I started to recite the Bible verse "though I walk through the valley of the shadow of death, I will fear no evil, for you are with me..." With those last comforting words, I was "out," and ready to go under the knife.

My surgery was a six-hour operation. I had my ribs drilled through and opened up. My heart was stopped for three hours as a heart-lung machine breathed for me and circulated my blood. The heart surgeon removed my entire aortic root and aortic valve and replaced it with a titanium aortic root and valve. Afterwards, I was told that the OR staff couldn't believe the extent the disease in my heart had deteriorated my aorta. To them, I was a walking miracle. To me, this news was God's confirmation that he had been taking care of me, especially considering I'd had no symptoms and my heart disease was found during a regular medical checkup. Fluke? Not according to my beliefs!

To them, I was a walking miracle.

As I recovered, people at the hospital heard of my faith and brought families to my hospital bed to pray for them. They wanted to experience the same peace God had given me as I walked through my own surgery.

My recovery was successful. It was a long journey, but I have lived to share my story. I am thankful I experienced the grace of God that carried me past the face of death because it has given me great confidence.

I needed that confidence to walk through horrific circumstances that could have destroyed my life. I know the enemy of our lives wants to bring destruction and we all are confronted with pain. I was raped, and then battled depression and an eating disorder. But with God, I am more than a conqueror. I can face anything in my life with him as my strength. The fear, pain, and intimidation cannot stay around when God heals our lives.

Realizing how precious and fragile life is, I decided to turn my pain into power. I decided to start *Unlock Magazine* to help hurting women and to inspire all women to live life to the fullest. Our pain in life can become our power when we overcome through the grace of God.

Katrina's story excites my heart. I love my wife and I see her as my hero! I admire her greatly for her faith and courage to press through the pain and the challenges, when it would have been easier to give up and become a victim. She is always looking to make a difference in people's lives.

Running a different direction

Many years ago, I had just bought myself a new pair of Nike shoes, and they were *nice*! I was driving down the road, and I saw a bearded homeless guy. He was pushing his cart along and I felt like God said, "Stop and talk to that guy. And give him your shoes."

I thought, uh-uh, I don't want to do that—that's not a God idea; that's a *bad* idea!

The thought came again, "Go over and talk to that guy."

So I pulled over to the side of the road and said, "Hey, how are you doing?"

He said, "My name's Henry."

I said, "May I buy you something to eat?" I thought he'd say, "Yeah, I want a Whopper."

But he said, "I'd like three Whoppers, a chicken sandwich, some fries, an apple fritter..." He just kept ordering!

I went over to Burger King, picked up all the food, and drove back. I felt like God said, "Put yourself in his shoes. I've enriched you to enrich other people; this isn't just about you."

So I sat down with him on the curb, and I said, "Henry, what do you want to do with your life?"

He said, "I'll tell you later."

"Well, what do you enjoy doing?"

"I'll tell you later."

I was thinking, man, this isn't making any sense. So then I said, "Henry, I want to tell you something. God's into giving people new beginnings in their lives. Would you mind if I put my shoes on your feet and you put your shoes on my feet? We will

God's into giving people new beginnings in their lives.

embrace each other's worlds. You'll begin to walk with a new life in your world."

He said, "Man, I'll take those shoes!"

I said, "Why don't you meet me at church tomorrow?"

The next day, he came to church and he had those new shoes on. After church, I took him to a buffet, and for two hours, the whole conversation was "I'll tell you about that later." I was thinking, man, this is an awful conversation; he doesn't answer anything I ask him.

But it was interesting that on that day, he opened up his heart to God, saying, "God, I want a new life," and only a couple months later, he was found dead.

Wow! That brought me to a standstill. What if I hadn't intersected with Henry's life? What if I'd been so focused on what I could get and on what I could do that I'd missed the opportunity to change someone's life forever?

One day when my time upon this planet is done, I will go to heaven and meet Jesus face to face. Right around the corner of heaven's gate, I know that I will see good ole bearded Henry and hear him say, "I'll tell you about that now."

Life can trap us in setbacks, getting us so focused on ourselves that all day long we walk past opportunities to make a difference and inspire people. Imagine how many people we go by every day, missing the opportunity to lift them.

Are you willing to raise your standard high enough to be the model that motivates others to notice and lift the people around them?

I honestly believe, you're the occasion for the event in someone's life. Your words will stimulate faith, lifting the potential and capability of another.

You're a miracle, a reward, and a hero to somebody on this planet.

The connection

Someone is waiting for you to take action so they can receive their miracle.

This concept grew in the mind of my good friend, Ben. After he heard me speak about it, he said it made so much sense, he began to put it into practice. Here is what happened:

As a school psychologist, I assist people on a daily basis. I am there to support students who are experiencing difficulties, whether they are academic, social, emotional, or behavioral in nature. One of my main roles is to provide assessments and make determinations for various learning disabilities. Although I am not a therapist, I do provide support for students who are experiencing emotional distress. When situations arise, I determine whether a student requires more in-depth attention than I can provide on a short-term basis.

After I had conducted an assessment of an eighth-grade Hispanic student for special education services, his mother called me. She was grateful for the academic support her son was receiving, but she was greatly distressed. Crying, she reported that he had expressed the desire to kill himself because he was unhappy with his life. She indicated that, on a few occasions, he had questioned why he was alive and wondered if it really mattered if he ended his life, since life "sucked" anyway. He expressed that he was just a burden to his mother who was already struggling to make ends meet financially and care for him and his brother. In his mind, suicide made sense because he would relieve his mother of any additional hardships, and he could avoid the continued struggles he was experiencing as a teenager in a gang-filled area.

After determining that he was not in immediate danger of taking his life, I began investing time in him and listening to his distress. We went through a few weeks of conversing, and each week it seemed as if he would make some headway; however, he would readily revert to suicidal thoughts after some other incident occurred or after he revisited those negative thoughts. He was in a very fragile state, wavering back and forth.

The tool that I found to be successful with him was not something I learned at a seminar or conference, or through one of many years of schooling, but a principle Rex taught at a Bible Study. As the student remained pessimistic and self-loathing, I presented to him what I had learned: "Don't you know that someone is waiting for you?" His immediate response was "Me? No, not me! I'm just a dumb kid. Why would anyone be waiting for me?"

"Don't you know that someone is waiting for you?"

I went on to explain that just as he had been waiting for me to come and assist him, that someone—maybe not tomorrow, maybe sometime far into the future—would be waiting for him. If he took his life, there would be a void and the person he was supposed to help would not receive that help. I further explained that he had a responsibility waiting for him in the future. Almost in an instant, those words seemed to permeate his mind and transform his thinking.

From that session on, our conversations took on a different tone. He began to question his previous thought process and seemed to take ownership of the new awareness that "someone is waiting for me." He began to challenge himself and look forward to what was ahead in his life. He seemed to be more inquisitive about how to make life better and how he could be an instrument of change in the world around him. Instead of being a statistic or a victim of his environment, he thought of ways he could become a vessel to make a difference in his world.

At this point, he was more optimistic and enjoying life. He would make statements about how he "used" to think and was glad that I was there to guide him. He soon began to refer other students to me who had expressed a similar disdain for life and negativity. I identified these individuals to him as the first ones to demonstrate that someone was indeed waiting for him.

At the end of the school year, we both marveled at how far he had progressed. He took the principles we had discussed and transformed his outlook on life by changing his mind-set.

It is one thing to know internally that you've made progress in your life, but when you are recognized by others, it solidifies that advancement and propels one even further. His graduation was his proudest moment because he was recognized for his academic achievements by receiving the highest achievement award available to middle school graduates. His teachers selected him from among a handful of students to receive the President of the United States Award for Achievement, signed by President Bush. This President's Award is handed out only to the elite of the elite of the school.

It was simply amazing that a Hispanic young man from a low socioeconomic area and a gang-infested environment, the son of a single mom, possessing a learning disability and emotional struggles, held on to a principle that propelled his life to a higher level. He was a student who, at the beginning of the year, didn't care about his life, let alone school, and who advanced himself by standing fast on that one concept, ultimately receiving one of the highest levels of achievement in his school.

He overcame all obstacles by changing the way he saw himself and by making a choice to fight for the future. He raised the awareness of the value of his life in this world and encompassed visions of a future that was unfathomable only months prior by grabbing a hold of God's Word. To this day, he continues to live by the principle of "someone is waiting for me." I don't cease to be amazed at the things God does in everyday individuals when they hold fast to his ways.

Releasing the hero within

Do you want more out of life? Life means risk, and if you have no risk in your current situation, that means you have no life. Unbelief is safe; it has no risk.

The truth is, your spirit craves adventure. Adventure describes the kind of life that awakened spirits are addicted to—a life of risk, reward, fortune, and faith. Without risk, you just have a scrapbook of moments you've collected on your journey as a remembrance of what you've done and where you've been.

But that was then, and this is now. Your potential, abilities, and dreams never came with a retirement plan. That's why you must respond to the intense desire inside you that says there's more to life than you've been living. If you want to become more, do more, and give more, it's because God is working inside of you so you become bigger, better, and brighter.

To go where you've never gone, you have to do something you've never done. You can watch things happen, you can make things happen, or you can wonder what happened.

It's time to have a love revolution in your life. It's time to deliver those who are drawn toward death. It's time to create a world of difference. It's time to leave a Jesus impression that reflects miracles, signs, and wonders.

To go where you've never gone, you have to do something you've never done.

The question is, when will you do it and how will you do it? Utilize God's power within. His power is always driven by love. Love always puts value on the despised, the unrecognized, the unnoticed, and the unlovable. It always searches for treasure, even in the midst of the trash.

Don't wait to get ahead in life; it's time to go ahead. Let the Spirit of God inside you turn the tide in somebody else's life. Take a risk—there's someone waiting for you! You're someone's hero.

Final Word

My life changed when I chose to become like-minded with God. I chose to start imitating the way he thinks, the way he speaks, and the way he loves. I encourage you to live in this revolutionary way, a way that will cause a life lift for you, and a life lifted for someone else.

Whatever happens, do something today. *This is your moment to master.*

To purchase books, for more information,
or to schedule Rex Crain to speak, please contact him at:

www.rexcrain.com

NOTES

Chapter 1

[1] T. D. Jakes, *Reposition Yourself* small devotional book preface.

Chapter 2

[1] Proverbs 23:7 The Amplified Bible

[2] Mark 9:23

[3] http://www.YouTube-Anthony Robbins.

[4] http://www.YouTube-Anthony Robbins.

[5] Isaiah 54:2

[6] Isaiah 43:18

[7] Micah 2:7 New King James Version

[8] Genesis 15:5

[9] Genesis 13:14-15

Chapter 3

[1] "An Incredibly Spiritual Woman," http://www.bspage.com/1article/peo19.html.

[2] Dr. Myles Munroe, *Releasing Your Potential: Exposing the Hidden You* (Shippensburg: Destiny Image, 1993).

[3] 2 Kings 4

[4] Genesis 10:8 King James Version

[5] Genesis 11:1-8

Chapter 4

[1] John C. Maxwell, *The 21 Irrefutable Laws of Leadership: Follow Them and People Will Follow You* (Nashville: Thomas Nelson, 1998).

2 Psalm 139:14 New International Version

3 Psalm 139:16 *New Living Translation*

4 Genesis 1:31 Amplified Bible

Chapter 5

1 Isaiah 49:16 New International Version

2 Psalm 139:17

3 Revelation 19:16, 1 Peter 2:9, Deuteronomy 28:13

4 *Merriam-Webster's Collegiate Dictionary*, 11th ed., s.v. "Broken."

5 Exodus 3

6 Judges 6:12 New King James Version

7 *Hitchcock's Bible Names Dictionary*, http://www2.mf.no/bibel/navn.html, s.v. "Gideon."

8 Judges 6:16

9 Jack Canfield, *The Success Principles: How to Get From Where You Are to Where You Want to Be* (New York: HarperResource, 2005).

Chapter 6

1 Anthony Robbins, *Awaken the Giant Within: How to Take Immediate Control of Your Mental, Emotional, Physical and Financial Destiny!* (New York: Free Press, 1992).

2 Joshua 24:15 New King James Version

3 Proverbs 12:11 *New Living Translation*

Chapter 7

1 Zechariah 4:10

Chapter 8

1 *Merriam-Webster's Collegiate Dictionary*, 11th ed., s.v. "Excellence."

2 Proverbs 3:35 *New Living Translation*

3 Proverbs 28:20 King James Version

Chapter 9

1 Matthew 14:17-21

2 Words: Proverbs 6:2; 11:11; 12:6,14; 15:1,4; 18:21; James 3:4-5; John 1:1

3 Proverbs 12:18 New International Version

4 Proverbs 12:25 New King James Version

5 Anthony Robbins, *Awaken the Giant Within: How to Take Immediate Control of Your Mental, Emotional, Physical and Financial Destiny!* (New York: Free Press, 1992).

Chapter 10

1 Psalm 43:5 New International Version

2 Romans 5:5 New International Version

3 *Merriam-Webster's Collegiate Dictionary,* 11th ed., s.v. "Bless."

4 Mark 11:22-23 New International Version

Chapter 13

1 Jeremiah 29:11 Amplified Bible

2 James 4:8 New King James Version

3 John 16:24 New King James Version

4 1 Corinthians 13

5 Genesis 9:18-27 Story of Noah

Chapter 14

1 Genesis 13:1-17 Story of Lot

2 Matthew 13: 54-55, 57-58 *New Living Translation*